FIFTY MORE FABLES OF LA FONTAINE

Fifty More Fables

of

La Fontaine

❦

Translated by
Norman R. Shapiro

Illustrations by
David Schorr

University of Illinois Press
Urbana and Chicago

*Publication of this book has been aided by a grant from
the Thomas and Catharine McMahon Fund, of Wesleyan University,
established through the generosity of the late Joseph McMahon.*

*This book was designed and typeset by David Schorr.
It is typeset in ITC Carter & Cone Galliard,
designed by Matthew Carter.*

This book is printed on acid-free paper.

Library of Congress Cataloging-in-Publication Data

La Fontaine, Jean de, 1621, 1695.
[Fables. English & French. Selections]
Fifty more fables of La Fontaine / translated by Norman R. Shapiro ;
illustrations by David Schorr.
p. cm.
Includes bibliographical references.
ISBN 0-252-02346-3 (cloth : alk. paper). —
ISBN 0-252-06650-2 (paper : alk. paper)
1. Fables, French—Translations into English.
I. Shapiro, Norman R. II. Schorr, David. III. Title.
PQ1811.E3S45 1998
841'.4—dc 21
96-49336
CIP

For Seymour O. Simches,
teacher, mentor, friend of many years

N.S.

For Phyllis Rose & Laurent de Brunhoff,

themselves a Franco-American fable

D.S.

CONTENTS

INTRODUCTION

Several years ago, in my introduction to *Fifty Fables of La Fontaine* (1988), I suggested that, somewhere down the line, another collection might well follow. At the time I had no specific plans to do one. But like criminals who always return to the scenes of their crimes, translators—for very different reasons, I hasten to add—always sooner or later return to their favorite authors. The year 1995 being a commemorative La Fontaine year—the 300th anniversary of his death—it seemed to me an auspicious moment to make good on that vague promise; and, as the year wore on, I became increasingly convinced that, if ever there was to be a time, this was indeed it. I could, of course, have decided to wait until the next appropriate date—the year 2021, the 400th anniversary of his birth—but that struck me as both presumptuous and impractical. (Besides, by that time people may no longer be reading translations of poetry—or poetry at all, for that matter—and if they are, what they read may well be computer generated, with no need for such as myself and like-crafted colleagues.) In September 1995, therefore, I decided that further delay was not recommended, and I set about translating the fables in the present collection.

My observations on La Fontaine's prestige as a preeminent fabulist, on his genius and geniality, and on the demands, challenges, and especially the pleasures inherent in transposing him into English verse, have not changed since *Fifty Fables*. To repeat them verbatim would be redundant; to paraphrase them would be an exercise in futility. After all, in the intervening years La Fontaine's position in French and world letters has not changed; either for the better (which would be impossible) or for the worse (which would be inconceivable). Readers, especially those for whom this volume is their first contact with the poet, are invited to refer to the *Fifty Fables* introduction. With the exception of a few additions to the bibliography, duly noted, what I wrote there is what I would also write here. For those unable to do so, however, and even for those who can, let me offer a brief poem written, insofar as my abilities would permit, in the manner of La Fontaine, in honor of this year commemorating his death, and giving at least a taste of the major elements of the subject matter, style, and influence of his prototypical *Fables*.

LA FONTAINE, LA SOURCE

His name was Jean de La Fontaine—or, rather, "is."
    For immortality is surely his:
        His name is *Jean de La Fontaine.*
    Three centuries have passed since his demise;
    And still he lives today no less than when
    His pen (or quill, I guess) would poetize
        A world of wily beasts (with men
            Now and again
    Thrown in—and women too: and even things!):
        And all the while, off in the wings
    (Or, often, center stage), himself, narrating,
        Commenting, quipping, explicating,
        Here with a wry grimace, there with a sly
            Wink of the eye,
    Digressing and expatiating
    (With many a casual parenthesis—
        Like this—)
    On flaws and foibles, frailties pananthropic,
    Of dramatis personæ *post-Æsopic.*
In short, a universe in verse! Verse "freed," not "free":
    Meters and rhymes—deft, spry, and sure,
    For all their bonne humeur *and* bonhomie,
    Their whimsy and désinvolture.
    Freedom within constraint: what art should be!
    For readers, now as then, what joy to see
    This fabled panorama, foible-rife,
        This universe of human flaws—
    Yet flawlessly portrayed—come spring to life!
        Yes, "spring to life" indeed, because
    "Spring" is the word when speaking of a source;
        Which is, of course,
    Just what a fountain is; and our Fontaine,
    No less than any other—even more—
    Deserves that meaning of his cognomen.
        That's not to say that, back before
He first put pen (no, quill!) to paper, to explore
    Man's vices with devices fabuliques—

Now with a twist linguistic, now a tweak
*   Of rhyme or rhythm—there had been*
No fabulists about to versify them;
Only that it was he who, to decry them,
First bent the shape that later poet-kin—
Successors (with much less success, despite
Their firm intent and not a little wit)—
Will do their best to follow; though as night
*   To day, their quill to his! For it*
*   Was not the fate, yearn though they might,*
Of any of the many a poetaster
*   To match the master!*
Still, try they did; most aping his technique
(Or close!); some working subjects he had wrought,
*   With morals changed; some proud to seek*
Out new ones that he had, himself, not sought;
Some crafting sequels, precious jeux d'esprit…
All questing their originality,
*   Anxious, indeed, lest they be thought*
"Influenced" by their fatherly castrator,
Cut down in fullest Bloom (if I may say,
Risking a dubious pun)…
*   Well, be that as it may,*
The question now remains for the translator,
*   How does one treat a prototype,*
*   A poet-creator of his stripe?*
One who defined a genre for all those
Who, in due reverence—or folly—chose
*   To try their hand—their quill? their pen?—*
And vie with him: la source, *La Fontaine?*

How does one do it? Heaven only knows!
But best I try to answer that in prose.[1]

That said (and read), a brief explication is in order to elucidate—
in prose, indeed—not only the problems facing the translator of
La Fontaine, as promised by the concluding couplet, but also the
essence of his art and craft; an explication that will expand on the

poem's three principal ideas: La Fontaine the narrator, La Fontaine the stylist, and La Fontaine the prototype.

As for La Fontaine the narrator, lines 10–17 sum up the pertinent characteristics rather succinctly ["And all the while, off in the wings / . . . (With many a casual parenthesis— / Like this—)"]. I might mention parenthetically in this regard that I was going, in fact, to entitle my poem *"Traduttore Seduttore,"* since good translators have to be seducers of sorts, have to exercise their "authorial power" to attract and retain the reader's attention. (I should really say "the listener's attention," because I am convinced that literature—all literature—is, or should be, written to be heard, even if only in the head, not merely scanned on paper: poetry especially, fables above all, and La Fontaine's even more than most.) But I soon realized that with La Fontaine one is much more the *sedotto* than the *seduttore*. It is quite impossible not to be "seduced" by his omnipresence as narrator: his friendly asides, his digressions, his confidences, his quips... In short, his personal contact with his reader/listener, his potential "receptor," if you will, over time and space. "He is," as I've written elsewhere, "always keenly aware of his readers . . . out there in the Great Literary Beyond, waiting to make eventual contact with them. And they, conversely, with him; which is easy to do since few authors, I think, establish as direct a rapport with their audience—a 'complicity' as I like to describe it."[2] Translating La Fontaine—an even more intimate association than merely reading him—is for me an act of pure hedonism. The *sedotto* willingly yields to the *seduttore*. That is why, for me at least, translating him is not only the expected exercise in re-creation that it is in all artistic translation but also and especially a supreme recreation: a pleasure or, in a word, fun. And that, thanks both to his pervasive and so very affable presence—omnipresence—as well as to the delights of his style that beg to be in some way duplicated, transposed, re-created in translation.

And so to La Fontaine the stylist, he of the *enjambements,* the rhymes—end-rhymes, inner rhymes—the assonances and echoes, the alliterations, the misplaced cæsuras (misplaced, but never lost!), the casual-appearing but still strictly countable meters, the verse freely flowing but still contained, still constrained but never strained, as lines 20–24 tell us [". . .Verse 'freed,' not 'free'. . . / Freedom within constraint: what art should be!"]. Quoting myself again, "This flexible form, with its profusion of run-on lines, internal rhymes, and natural speech rhythms, afforded La Fontaine the perfect compromise between the poet's innate need for verse and the storyteller's need for the naturalness of prose. The resulting tension between freedom and constraint is one of the greatest charms of his work."[3] Now, if I wanted to wax philosophical and theoretical, I might point out to what extent this is a microcosm, of sorts, of Man's very being; no less than an expression of the struggle between Free Will and Determinism: his dual and contradictory desires for total freedom, on the one hand, and total dependency, on the other; the latter being what the psychoanalyst Erich Fromm, years ago, in a very particular context, perceptively dubbed the "escape from freedom." I might even point out how the very act of translation itself is also an expression of this duality, a satisfying compromise between these two "tugs" of Man's nature: the translator, safe from the fearsome total freedom of the blank page, is securely bound to the text, circumscribed by its constraints, yet at the same time so very free within them. "Freedom within constraint" indeed...

But let me not digress, fitting though digression is in any discussion of La Fontaine. As I've said, I changed my title. By a happy and appropriate coincidence, the French *fontaine* and *source* are, like their English counterparts, synonymous. And certainly when it comes to post-Æsopic practitioners of the verse fable, La Fontaine, to quote lines 30–34, is *the* source par excellence [" 'Spring' is the word when speaking of a source: / Which is, of course, / Just what a fountain is; and our Fontaine, / No less than any other—even more— / Deserves that meaning of his cognomen"]. Which is not to suggest that our poet was the originator of the genre in France. Indeed, his medieval and Renaissance predecessors were many, albeit there is some debate as to how many of them were even known to him. At any rate, as lines 41–49 affirm ["Only that it was he . . . / To match the master!"], it was La Fontaine and not the likes of Deschamps, Corrozet, Haudent, Guéroult, Baïf, Hégémon, *et al.*—or even the admirable Marie de France, medieval creator of the genre—who set the pace that his legion of successors were to follow. And, as we know, follow they did; some fairly dogging his tracks, others at more respectable distances.[4] Indeed, for most he may as well have been the first, so appropriate was the mold that he cast for the genre; and so pervasive his influence, even, paradoxically, among those who seemed bent on avoiding it. For all he remains—whether acknowledged or not—the point of reference; to try to absent him is merely to reaffirm his presence.

Clearly there is no need to prove that influence on La Fontaine's fabulist successors, even deep into our own century, whether they admit or deny it, and however much their own quest for artistic originality might color their work. Lines 55–58 speak to the point with theoretical allusion ["All questing their originality . . . / Cut down in fullest Bloom . . ."].

> But however obviously they flatter him by imitation, or however sincere their praise and deep their salaams at the shrine of his incomparability, they must all, it seems to me, be of two minds in the matter, realize it or not. In a literary love-hate relationship, as it were. With filial affection for their spiritual progenitor, on the one hand, and resentment at the same time—in Bloomian terms—toward the all-powerful and threatening castrating Fabulist-Father, on the other. "Also-rans" by definition and condemned to remain such, they are caught (if I may make a pun) between their cerebral urge to run toward him in love and their visceral urge to run from him in hate.[5]

To fulfill the promise of my poem's conclusion, a few words are in order about the "how" of translating La Fontaine. (It would be equally pertinent to discuss the "why" of translating him—and of literary translation in general—had I not already made clear my own unabashed hedonism. Suffice it to add the observation made on other occasions, but always worth repeating, that translators must have something of the masochist about them, given the short shrift they generally receive in the world of letters—if, that is, they receive any shrift at all. Be that as it may...) One must assume, first, that it is, in fact, possible to translate poetry. Some—Yves Bonnefoy is a good example—hold that to translate poetry is basically an impossibility. Perhaps, but only if one means the kind of often hermetic, semantically and interpretationally multilayered works meant more to be read on the page and pondered over—pored over and deciphered—than to be heard and immediately comprehended. La Fontaine, thank heaven, is a purveyor of the latter. Translating him is a challenge, to be sure, but a delightful and rewarding one.[6]

Simplistically speaking, the challenge is to reproduce in English both "the tune and the tone," to quote Seamus Heaney. The story and the style. How does a translator bring across both? Some, who have no trouble with the former, fall woefully short when it comes to the latter. Indeed, some don't even bother to try; for them it's only the tune that counts. "But for those of us who take the job seriously, the tone is no less a part of the original, and somehow it must be rendered if we are going to re-create it. We may not always succeed, but at least we know enough to make the attempt. As for how it's done, while the tune can be taught and learned, the tone, I suspect, is a matter of intuition."[7] A matter, in La Fontaine's case, of maintaining in English, without being shackled to a line-for-line correspondence, certainly—and by some indefinable alchemy that requires more than a good thesaurus and rhyming dictionary—that easygoing, often chatty *désinvolture* of La Fontaine's "freed" verse: the freedom within form, the flow, the cadence; the asides, digressions, pauses often as pregnant as what precedes and follows, the collusions with the reader, present and future; the color of his language, the occasional archaism... In short, all the elements that make up the "tone" and that all must be incorporated, somehow, when we translate the works of our prototype, our *source:* our La Fontaine.

> *His name is Jean de La Fontaine;*
> *His likes will, likely, not be heard again.*

A trio of good friends has attended the birth of this offspring, like that of several of its elders. To them—Evelyn Singer Simha, Caldwell Titcomb, and Lillian Bulwa—my appreciation for useful suggestion, willing ear, and unstinting encouragement.

Thanks, too, to Alan Hartford, but for whom it might not have seen the light; to Sylvia and Allan Kliman, for valued support and constant concern; to Adams House, Harvard University, in the persons of Robert and Jana Kiely, and Vicki (alias Tori) Macy, for much sustenance—intellectual and other—during its gestation; to Elizabeth Dulany, Pat Hollahan, Theresa Sears, Cope Cumpston, and their colleagues at the University of Illinois Press, for their expert midwifery; to Mary Shea and Beardsley Ruml III, for technical assistance and advice with the delivery; to Rita Dempsey and Carla Chrisfield, for getting their fax straight; to Clifford Landers, for much generous interest; and to Connie Lee, for ambience, coffee, and a beehive of good cheer.

As ever, no volume of my verse would be complete without my acknowledging a debt to my late mother, from whom I first learned the reason of rhyme, and whose example continues to teach me.

And, of course, a special bravo to David Schorr, for his always splendid artwork and indispensable collaboration.

NOTES

1 These verses were written as part of a paper delivered at the Jean de La Fontaine International Colloquium, Hunter College, City University of New York, April 12 and 13, 1995.

2 *La Fontaine's Bawdy: Of Libertines, Louts, and Lechers* (translations from his *Contes et nouvelles en vers*) (Princeton: Princeton University Press, 1992), p. xviii.

3 *Fifty Fables of La Fontaine*, trans. Norman R. Shapiro (Urbana: University of Illinois Press, 1988), p. xiv.

4 Regarding La Fontaine's predecessors and his numerous successors, with translations from their works, see my volume *The Fabulists French: Verse Fables of Nine Centuries* (Urbana: University of Illinois Press, 1992).

5 Shapiro, *The Fabulists French*, p. xiv. The reader will recognize my allusion to Harold Bloom's thesis in his—influential—volume *The Anxiety of Influence: A Theory of Poetry* (New York: Oxford University Press, 1973).

6 See my article "Climbing Mt. La Fontaine," *ATA Source* (newsletter of the literary division of the American Translators Association), Fall 1995, pp. 1, 12–15.

7 *Fifty Fables of La Fontaine*, p. xiv.

BIBLIOGRAPHY

The single most authoritative work in the La Fontaine corpus continues to be the exhaustively (and exhaustingly) annotated eleven-volume critical edition of Henri Regnier, *Œuvres de J. de la Fontaine,* rev. ed. (Paris: Hachette, 1883–92), in the series "Les Grands Ecrivains de la France." For reasons of convenience, however, I have chosen rather to reproduce here Ferdinand Gohin's less typographically cumbersome French text of the *Fables* as it appears in the Association Guillaume Budé's two-volume edition, complete despite its title's apparent implication. The *Fables choisies mises en vers* (Paris: Société des Belles Lettres, 1934) purports to be a faithful reproduction of the last edition corrected by the poet himself, and I reproduce it with all its vagaries of seventeenth-century orthography and punctuation, altering only a few apparent misprints.

As for secondary works in the La Fontaine bibliography, vast and constantly growing, I shall mention here, as in *Fifty Fables of La Fontaine,* only those readily available book-length studies in English:

Jean Dominique Biard, *The Style of La Fontaine's "Fables"* (Oxford: Blackwell, 1966)

Richard Danner, *Patterns of Irony in the "Fables" of La Fontaine* (Athens: Ohio University Press, 1985)

Margaret Guiton, *La Fontaine, Poet and Counterpoet* (New Brunswick, N.J.: Rutgers University Press, 1961)

Frank Hamel, *Jean de La Fontaine* (London: Stanley Paul, 1911; rpt., Port Washington, N.Y.: Kennikat Press, 1970)

Ethel M. King, *Jean de La Fontaine* (Brooklyn: Gaus, 1970)

David Lee Rubin, *A Pact with Silence: Art and Thought in the Fables of Jean de La Fontaine* (Columbus: Ohio State University Press, 1991)

Agnes Ethel Mackey, *La Fontaine and His Friends* (New York: Braziller, 1973)

Monica Sutherland, *La Fontaine* (London: Jonathan Cape, 1953; rpt., London: Jonathan Cape, 1974)

Marie-Odile Sweetser, *La Fontaine* (Boston: Twayne, 1987)

Michael Vincent, *Figures of the Text: Reading and Writing in La Fontaine* (Amsterdam and Philadelphia: John Benjamin, 1992)

Philip Wadsworth, *Young La Fontaine* (Evanston, Ill.: Northwestern University Press, 1952)

The following, while devoted primarily to La Fontaine's less generally well-known *Contes* (1665–74), contains stylistic observations applicable as well to his *Fables:*

John Clarke Lapp, *The Esthetics of Negligence: La Fontaine's "Contes"* (Cambridge: Cambridge University Press, 1971)

FIFTY MORE FABLES OF LA FONTAINE

LE LOUP ET LE CHIEN

Un Loup n'avoit que les os et la peau;
   Tant les Chiens faisoient bonne garde.
Ce Loup rencontre un Dogue aussi puissant que beau,
Gras, poli, qui s'estoit fourvoyé par mégarde.
   L'attaquer, le mettre en quartiers,
   Sire Loup l'eust fait volontiers.
   Mais il falloit livrer bataille;
   Et le Mâtin estoit de taille
   A se défendre hardiment.
   Le Loup donc l'aborde humblement,
Entre en propos, et luy fait compliment
   Sur son embonpoint qu'il admire:
   Il ne tiendra qu'à vous, beau Sire,
D'estre aussi gras que moy, luy repartit le Chien.

THE WOLF AND THE HOUND

A wolf there was, grown wan and thin;
   Little, indeed, but bone and skin,
So staunchly did the watchdogs do their duty.
   At length a hound strays by his lair—
   Sleek, fat, and passing debonair,
And no less well endowed of strength than beauty.
   Happily would Sire Wolf attack him,
      Pummel him, thwack him,
      Hack him to bits.
Ah, but to do so meant that he must fight;
   And clearly they would not be quits
   Before Sire Mastiff—able (quite!)
   To hold his own—might lay him low!
And so our wolf draws near, in humblest wise,
Flatters his plump and portly bearing. "Oh?"

Quittez les bois, vous ferez bien:
Vos pareils y sont miserables,
Cancres, haires, et pauvres diables,
Dont la condition est de mourir de faim.
Car quoy? Rien d'assuré; point de franche lipée:
Tout à la pointe de l'épée.
Suivez-moy; vous aurez un bien meilleur destin.
Le Loup reprit: Que me faudra-t-il faire?
—Presque rien, dit le Chien, donner la chasse aux gens
Portans bastons et mendians;
Flater ceux du logis, à son Maistre complaire;
Moyennant quoy vostre salaire
Sera force reliefs de toutes les façons:
Os de poulets, os de pigeons:
Sans parler de mainte caresse.
Le Loup déja se forge une felicité
Qui le fait pleurer de tendresse.
Chemin faisant il vid le col du Chien pelé.
Qu'est-ce là? luy dit-il.—Rien.—Quoy rien?—Peu de chose.
—Mais encor?—Le colier dont je suis attaché
De ce que vous voyez est peut-estre la cause.
—Attaché? dit le Loup; vous ne courez donc pas
Où vous voulez?—Pas toûjours, mais qu'importe?
—Il importe si bien, que de tous vos repas
Je ne veux en aucune sorte,
Et ne voudrois pas mesme à ce prix un tresor.
Cela dit, Maistre Loup s'enfuit, et court encor.

Replies the hound. "If you admire my size,
    The choice is yours, good sire. If you
Would fatten up like me, do as I do:
Come, leave this dire and deadly wood behind.
What good does it do you and all your kind?
    Poor devils, starving wretches, who
Ever must brave the blade for every crumb,
    Never to feast their fill! Come, come...
    A fairer fate awaits." "But... But,"
Queries the wolf, "what must I do?" "'What?... What?'"
Echoes the hound. "Why, almost nothing, friend:
Chase away beggars, churls with sticks... Attend
The household folk... Do all you can to please
    The master... In return for which
    Fine table scraps—delicacies
    Of every sort—will be your rich
Reward: squab bones, and chicken bones, and such...
    What's more, you'll know the loving touch
Of master's fond caress." The wolf, thereat,
Weeps at the happy thought. But, on their way,
He spies the hound's bald neck. "What's that, I pray?"
"This what?" "That!" "This?... Why, nothing!" "'Nothing?' That?..."
"Almost, that is... It's where my collar sits.
The one they use to tie me down. It fits
A trifle snug." "'Tie down?' Then you're not free?
You can't go where you choose, run where you will?"
    "Not always. But who cares?" "Who? Me!
Keep your fine feasts! I'll keep my liberty!"
Whereat our wolf went running off. He's running still.

(I, 5)

LA GENISSE, LA CHEVRE, ET LA BREBIS
EN SOCIETE AVEC LE LION

La Genisse, la Chevre et leur sœur la Brebis
Avec un fier Lion, Seigneur du voisinage,
Firent société, dit-on, au temps jadis,
Et mirent en commun le gain et le dommage.
Dans les laqs de la Chevre un Cerf se trouva pris.
Vers ses associez aussi-tost elle envoye.
Eux venus, le Lion par ses ongles conta,
Et dit: Nous sommes quatre à partager la proye;
Puis en autant de parts le Cerf il dépeça,
Prit pour luy la première en qualité de Sire:
Elle doit estre à moy, dit-il, et la raison,
  C'est que je m'appelle Lion:
  A cela l'on n'a rien à dire.
La seconde par droit me doit échoir encor:
Ce droit, vous le sçavez, c'est le droit du plus fort.
Comme le plus vaillant je prétens la troisième.
Si quelqu'une de vous touche à la quatrième,
  Je l'étrangleray tout d'abord.

THE HEIFER, THE GOAT, AND THE LAMB
IN CONSORT WITH THE LION

In ages past, they say, the sisterhood
Of heifer, goat, and lamb kept company
With lion, the haughty monarch of the wood,
Sharing life's weal and woe, bad times and good.
One day the goat, discovering that she
Had snared herself a stag, sent presently
For her companions, who arrived straightway.
The lion, counting on his paws, declared:
"Let now the four of us mete out our prey!"
    That said, the king of beasts prepared
To hack the stag in quarters. "There!" said he.
"Now then, the first part surely goes to me,
    Lion by name, your sovereign. Who,
Indeed, would dare dispute with me my due?
By right the next is mine as well; for might,
    As often one observes, makes right.
Valor deserves the third: I'll take that too.
    As for the fourth... Since, forasmuch, it
Must be the last, I'll kill the first to touch it!"

(I, 6)

L'HOMME ENTRE DEUX AGES ET SES DEUX MAISTRESSES

Un homme de moyen âge,
Et tirant sur le grison,
Jugea qu'il étoit saison
De songer au mariage.
Il avoit du contant,
Et partant
Dequoy choisir. Toutes vouloient luy plaire;
En quoy nostre amoureux ne se pressoit pas tant.
Bien adresser n'est pas petite affaire.
Deux veuves sur son cœur eurent le plus de part:
L'une encor verte, et l'autre un peu bien mûre,
Mais qui reparoit par son art
Ce qu'avoit détruit la nature.
Ces deux Veuves, en badinant,
En riant, en luy faisant feste,

THE MIDDLE-AGED MAN AND HIS TWO MISTRESSES

A man of middling age, one day,
　　Decides the time has come,
Now growing grizzled—nay, grown gray!—
　　To end his bachelordom.
Wealthy he is, and prosperous.
　　　　And thus
The pick (or so to speak) is his: in sum,
Women galore would be his bride. They yearn
　　To earn his favor. He, in turn,
　　Knows that, in love, the choice is slow;
Knows he must ponder every *con* and *pro*
Before deciding... Now, of those who burn
　　To win his heart, two widows stand
Above the rest; one, fresh and green, the other... Well,
　　More ripe; but, wonderful to tell,
　　Able, with art, to mend what nature's hand
Has cruelly rent asunder... Widows, they,

L'alloient quelquefois testonnant,
C'est à dire ajustant sa teste.
La Vieille à tous momens de sa part emportoit
Un peu du poil noir qui restoit,
Afin que son amant en fust plus à sa guise.
La Jeune saccageoit les poils blancs à son tour.
Toutes deux firent tant que nostre teste grise
Demeura sans cheveux, et se douta du tour.
Je vous rends, leur dit-il, mille graces, les Belles,
Qui m'avez si bien tondu;
J'ay plus gagné que perdu:
Car d'Hymen, point de nouvelles.
Celle que je prendrois voudroit qu'à sa façon
Je vécusse, et non à la mienne.
Il n'est teste chauve qui tienne,
Je vous suis obligé, Belles, de la leçon.

Who fawned and frolicked, and—one used to say—
"Coifed" him betimes. (A word not often said
Today, but one that meant "to groom the head.")
The older one, for her part, pulled the few
    Dark hairs that, here and there, still grew
    About his scalp, so that monsieur
Might look to be a bit more fit for her.
    Likewise, the younger, thereunto,
Plucked all the white as well. Duly appalled,
Monsieur, at length—no longer gray—was bald.
    "My dears," said he, "though high the cost,
    Truly, more have I gained than lost.
Marriage is not for me, I fear. A wife
    Would want me not to live my life,
But hers. And though, of late, my pate is bare,
Thank you, my loves. The lesson's worth my hair."

(I, 17)

LE RENARD ET LA CIGOGNE

Compere le Renard se mit un jour en frais,
Et retint à disner commere la Cigogne.
Le régal fut petit, et sans beaucoup d'apprests;
　　Le galand pour toute besogne
Avoit un broüet clair (il vivoit chichement).
Ce broüet fut par luy servy sur une assiette:
La Cigogne au long bec n'en put attraper miette;
Et le drôle eut lapé le tout en un moment.
　　Pour se vanger de cette tromperie,
A quelque temps de là, la Cigogne le prie.
Volontiers, luy dit-il, car avec mes amis
　　Je ne fais point ceremonie.
　　A l'heure dite il courut au logis

THE FOX AND THE STORK

One day Renard, the fox—goodfellow he!—
    Extends his hospitality
To Goodwife Stork, inviting her to dinner.
    Scant is the fare (no spendthrift sinner
This fox of ours!): only a thinnish gruel—
Thinner than thin—served in a shallow dish.
Long as she is of bill, dear though her wish
To sup, the stork gives up, gulled by his cruel
    And crafty hoax. Renard, thereat,
Laps, guzzles, gulps it down with ease. But later
The joke's on him: she gives him tit for tat,
Inviting him in turn. Our witful traitor,
Quick to accept, replies: *"Merci beaucoup!*
    Away, madame, with false pretense—
No need for tra-la-la with friends like you."

De la Cigogne son hôtesse,
Loüa tres-fort la politesse,
Trouva le disner cuit à point.
Bon appetit sur tout; Renards n'en manquent point.
Il se réjoüissoit à l'odeur de la viande
Mise en menus morceaux, et qu'il croyoit friande.
On servit, pour l'embarasser,
En un vase à long col, et d'étroite embouchure.
Le bec de la Cigogne y pouvoit bien passer,
Mais le museau du Sire estoit d'autre mesure.
Il luy falut à jeun retourner au logis,
Honteux comme un Renard qu'une Poule auroit pris,
Serrant la queüe, et portant bas l'oreille.
Trompeurs, c'est pour vous que j'écris,
Attendez-vous à la pareille.

And so, come eve, off to her residence
He flies; arrives; flatters her gracious air;
    Spies the repast; sniffles its scents;
Ogles the chunks of meat, minced fine, spread there
    Before his hungering eyes; delights
In one of those uncommon appetites
    Common to foxes!... Ah, but lo!
Stork serves them in a long vase, narrow-necked.
Her thin, sharp beak fits snugly in. But oh!
Our hero's snout is, as you might suspect,
Quite the wrong shape and size! So, eating crow,
Like fox outwitted by the chicken coop,
    Shamefaced, abject, ears all a-droop,
Tail tucked betwixt his legs, home will he go,
    Outdone, unfed... outfoxed! Indeed,
Tricksters, you could be next: hear, and take heed!

                      (I, 18)

L'ENFANT ET LE MAISTRE D'ECOLE

Dans ce recit je pretens faire voir
D'un certain sot la remontrance vaine.
Un jeune enfant dans l'eau se laissa choir,
En badinant sur les bords de la Seine.
Le Ciel permit qu'un saule se trouva
Dont le branchage, aprés Dieu, le sauva.
S'estant pris, dis-je, aux branches de ce saule,
Par cet endroit passe un Maistre d'école.
L'enfant luy crie: Au secours, je peris!
Le Magister, se tournant à ses cris,
D'un ton fort grave à contre-temps s'avise
De le tancer: Ah! le petit baboüin!
Voyez, dit-il, où l'a mis sa sotise!
Et puis prenez de tels fripons le soin.
Que les parens sont malheureux, qu'il faille
Toûjours veiller à semblable canaille!
Qu'ils ont de maux! et que je plains leur sort!
Ayant tout dit, il mit l'enfant à bord.
Je blâme icy plus de gens qu'on ne pense.
Tout babillard, tout censeur, tout pedant,
Se peut connoistre au discours que j'avance:
Chacun des trois fait un peuple fort grand;
Le Createur en a beny l'engeance.
En toute affaire ils ne font que songer
    Aux moyens d'exercer leur langue.
Hé mon amy, tire-moy de danger:
    Tu feras aprés ta harangue.

THE CHILD AND THE SCHOOLMASTER

I tell the present fable to portray
The arrant folly of a babbling sot
Whose wont it was to twaddle time away...
Well then, my tale. One day a child at play
Chanced to fall in the Seine. But it was not,
Praise Heaven! his fate to sink: a willow limb—
At God's behest!—hung low and succored him.
Seizing the branch, the poor tot clutched it fast...
As there he clung among the boughs, there passed
A pedant sort, schoolmaster by vocation.
"Help!" yelps the child. "I'm dead!" The *magister*,
Deciding that a proper remonstration
Is what the urchin needs, stops then and there
And, with his most censorious, priggish air,
Proceeds to censure him. "You little minx!
See where your foolish mischief leads? Methinks,
My imp, you'll learn your lesson!... Ha! Go try
To care for scamps and knaves like these! My eye!
God help their parents! What a cross have they
To bear, day out, day in! Alackaday!..."
At length he pulls the youngster out. But, ah!
Not before many a "Bah!" *et cætera*...
　　Several the laughingstocks of mine
Depicted here; more than you think: the scold,
The pedant, and the chatterbox. Untold
　　Their numbers! God has blessed their line.
Tongue-waggers, one and all! My prattling prater,
Rescue me first; give me your lecture later!

(I, 19)

LA LICE ET SA COMPAGNE

Une Lice estant sur son terme,
Et ne sçachant où mettre un fardeau si pressant,
Fait si bien qu'à la fin sa Compagne consent
De luy prêter sa hute, où la Lice s'enferme.
Au bout de quelque temps sa Compagne revient.
La Lice luy demande encore une quinzaine.
Ses petits ne marchoient, disoit-elle, qu'à peine.
Pour faire court, elle l'obtient.
Ce second terme échû, l'autre luy redemande
Sa maison, sa chambre, son lit.
La Lice cette fois montre les dents, et dit:
Je suis prête à sortir avec toute ma bande,
Si vous pouvez nous mettre hors.
Ses enfans étoient déja forts.

Ce qu'on donne aux méchans, toûjours on le regrette.
Pour tirer d'eux ce qu'on leur prête,
Il faut que l'on en vienne aux coups;
Il faut plaider, il faut combattre.
Laissez-leur prendre un pied chez vous,
Ils en auront bien-tôt pris quatre.

THE MASTIFF BITCH AND HER FRIEND

A mastiff bitch, about to bear her litter,
Not knowing where to lay her pressing load,
Implores a friend, who says she will permit her,
Presently, to make use of her abode.
When all is said and done, the latter bitch
Returns, requests her habitat; at which,
"A fortnight more," the mother begs her. "Please!
　Two weeks! My pups can scarcely walk!"
Whereat the other, touched by all her talk—
　To make our story short—agrees.
　Said time elapses, and again
The friend would claim her home, her room, her bed.
"Never!" the disingenuous quadruped
Replies, fangs bared. "I'll vacate only when
You think you're big enough to kick us out!"
Needless to say, her pups had grown quite stout.

　Lend to the wicked and regret it!
　(Alas, that's what this tale's about.)
　You'll ask it back but never get it:
　　You'll fight, you'll sue...
　Do what you might, do what you do;
　No matter: give a finger... and
　　They take a hand.

(II, 7)

LE LION ET LE RAT &
LA COLOMBE ET LA FOURMY

Il faut autant qu'on peut obliger tout le monde:
On a souvent besoin d'un plus petit que soy.
De cette verité deux Fables feront foy,
  Tant la chose en preuves abonde.

  Entre les pattes d'un Lion
Un Rat sortit de terre assez à l'étourdie.
Le Roy des animaux, en cette occasion,
Montra ce qu'il estoit, et luy donna la vie.
  Ce bienfait ne fut pas perdu.
  Quelqu'un auroit-il jamas crû
  Qu'un Lion d'un Rat eût affaire?
Cependant il avint qu'au sortir des forests
  Ce lion fut pris dans des rets
Dont ses rugissemens ne le pûrent défaire.
Sire Rat accourut, et fit tant par ses dents
Qu'une maille rongée emporta tout l'ouvrage.
  Patience et longueur de temps
  Font plus que force ny que rage.

L'autre exemple est tiré d'animaux plus petits.
Le long d'un clair ruisseau beuvoit une Colombe,
Quand sur l'eau se panchant une Fourmy y tombe;
Et dans cet Ocean l'on eust vû la Fourmy
S'efforcer, mais en vain, de regagner la rive.
La Colombe aussi-tost usa de charité:
Un brin d'herbe dans l'eau par elle estant jetté,
Ce fut un promontoire où la Fourmy arrive.
  Elle se sauve; et là-dessus
Passe un certain Croquant qui marchoit les pieds nus.
Ce Croquant par hazard avoit une arbaleste.
  Dés qu'il void l'Oiseau de Venus,
Il le croit en son pot, et déja luy fait feste.
Tandis qu'à le tuer mon Villageois s'appreste,
  La Fourmy le pique au talon.
  Le Vilain retourne la teste.
La Colombe l'entend, part, et tire de long.
Le souper du Croquant avec elle s'envole:
  Point de Pigeon pour une obole.

THE LION AND THE RAT &
THE DOVE AND THE ANT

Man should serve everyone as best he's able.
 Often, however great we be,
We need the help of lesser folk than we.
The proof abounds: witness my double fable.

A certain rat—a bumbling sort he was—
Came stumbling from his hole, only to find
 Himself betwixt a lion's paws!
The kingly beast was nonetheless inclined
(At least this time) to do a kindly deed.
 He let him go; most *beau* the *geste!*
 Nor was it lost. Who could have guessed
 That one fine day a lion would need
 A rat to save his skin! And yet
It happened that our generous liberator,
Leaving his lair, got tangled in a net...
He roars, he struggles... All for nought. But later,
Who comes? Sire Rat! He sees him, hears his cries;
 Nibbles one stitch; and, little wonder,
Gnaws it so well, the rest comes all asunder.
Patience works more than rage; time, more than size.[1]

My other tale, unlike the one above,
Tells of two beasts of smallish size: a dove—
 The first—was drinking from a brook;
An ant—the second—there as well, mistook
Her distance; leaned too far; and in she fell.
Were one to look one would have seen the ant
Struggling against the ocean's swirl and swell
 To reach the shore... Alas, she can't.
Of generous bent, the dove at once lays out
 A blade of grass (so goes the story)—
 A veritable promontory!—
Whereby the ant is saved... Now, thereabout,
A certain barefoot bumpkin, sling in hand,
 By chance comes by; and, straightway spying
Venus's sacred bird,[2] he stands there, eyeing
Covetously his feast... But as he planned
 To make said fowl his evening meal,
 The ant went nipping at his heel:
Churl starts... Dove hears, flies off... Our village sinner
Watches her go, and bids adieu to dinner.

(II, 11, 12)

LE CORBEAU VOULANT IMITER L'AIGLE

L'Oyseau de Jupiter enlevant un Mouton,
        Un Corbeau témoin de l'affaire,
Et plus foible de reins, mais non pas moins glouton,
        En voulut sur l'heure autant faire.
        Il tourne à l'entour du troupeau,
Marque entre cent Moutons le plus gras, le plus beau,
        Un vray Mouton de sacrifice:
On l'avoit reservé pour la bouche des Dieux.
Gaillard Corbeau disoit, en le couvant des yeux:
        Je ne sçay qui fut ta nourrice,
Mais ton corps me paroist en merveilleux état:
        Tu me serviras de pâture.

THE CROW WHO WANTED TO IMITATE THE EAGLE

An eagle—sacred bird of Jove—
Soaring the sky, went swooping, dove,
Snatched up a sheep and bore him off. Hard by,
A crow looked on with envious eye—
Though less robust, not one whit less the glutton!—
Thinking he too might snare his share of mutton.
Circling above the flock, said crow surveyed
The five score sheep below, and made
His choice; it took him not a trice
To find the finest, plumpest of the lot:
A fresh young lamb, fit for the sacrifice,
Food for the gods. "Ah, tender tot!"
Observed our ravening *bon vivant*. "I know
Not who it was that suckled you. But what

Sur l'animal beslant, à ces mots, il s'abat.
      La Moutonniere creature
Pesoit plus qu'un fromage; outre que sa toison
      Estoit d'une épaisseur extrême,
Et meslée à peu prés de la mesme façon
      Que la barbe de Polipheme.
Elle empestra si bien les serres du Corbeau
Que le pauvre animal ne put faire retraite;
Le Berger vient, le prend, l'encage bien et beau,
Le donne à ses enfans pour servir d'amusette.
Il faut se mesurer, la consequence est nette.
Mal prend aux Volereaux de faire les Voleurs.
      L'exemple est un dangereux leure:
Tous les mangeurs de gens ne sont pas grands Seigneurs;
Où la Guespe a passé, le Moucheron demeure.

A specimen you are!... That being so,
Prepare to be my meal." Wherewith the crow
Swoops low to seize him... Sheepdom's pride is not,
Alas, an easy prey: more does he weigh
Than, say, crow's usual cheese! Besides, unsheared,
His fleece is thick as Polyphemus' beard,[1]
   All snarl and knot!... Alackaday,
   Claws caught, stuck fast, there will he stay
Until the shepherd comes. He frees him, takes him
   Home to his children, caged, and makes him
Nought but a silly pet!... Ah! What fools we,
Not to resist the lure of mimicry;
   To ape our betters. Whence, infer:
Best know our limits; petty thieves should be
   Content with petty thievery.
Not all who feed on man are fine *seigneurs:*
The gnat remains entrapped; the wasp flies free.

(II, 16)

LE PAON SE PLAIGNANT A JUNON

Le Paon se plaignoit à Junon:
Deesse, disoit-il, ce n'est pas sans raison
Que je me plains, que je murmure:
Le chant dont vous m'avez fait don
Déplaist à toute la Nature;
Au lieu qu'un Rossignol, chetive creature,
Forme des sons aussi doux qu'éclatans,
Est luy seul l'honneur du Printemps.
Junon répondit en colere:
Oyseau jaloux, et qui devrois te taire,
Est-ce à toy d'envier la voix du Rossignol,
Toy que l'on voit porter à l'entour de ton col
Un arc-en-ciel nué de cent sortes de soyes;
Qui te panades, qui déployes
Une si riche queuë, et qui semble à nos yeux
La Boutique d'un Lapidaire?
Est-il quelque oyseau sous les Cieux
Plus que toy capable de plaire?
Tout animal n'a pas toutes proprietez.
Nous vous avons donné diverses qualitez:
Les uns ont la grandeur et la force en partage;
Le Faucon est leger, l'Aigle plein de courage;
Le Corbeau sert pour le présage,
La Corneille avertit des malheurs à venir;
Tous sont contens de leur ramage.
Cesse donc de te plaindre, ou bien, pour te punir,
Je t'osteray ton plumage.

THE PEACOCK WHO COMPLAINED TO JUNO

The peacock, once, went grumbling his lament
To Juno: "Goddess, hear my discontent.
Reason enough have I for my displeasure.
This voice you gave me, shrill beyond all measure,
Makes all of Nature quiver, quake, and quail.
    Whereas you made the nightingale—
    Poor, puny creature that he is!—
Able to please—nay, captivate—with his.
His song alone pays homage to the Spring."
Vexed, Juno answered: "Oh, you envious thing!
You, with your silken, rainbow-splendored tail,
Shimmering, halo-like, about your head!
    You, jealous of the nightingale?
His voice? You? You, who strut, and preen, and spread
Those beauteous hues? Why, we would think that we
    Were in a jeweler's shop, to see
    Such finery as yours! Is there
    A beast who, therebelow, would dare
Boast that he pleases more than you? I doubt it!
To each some special trait, some quality:
But no bird has them all, no doubt about it!
Lightness of wing, the hawk; the eagle, bravery;
    The gift of prophecy, raven and crow,
    To warn man of impending woe...
    Yet one and all find nothing wrong
With what I've given them to sing their song.
So stop your whining, lest I punish you:
Leave you your voice... and pluck your feathers too!"

(II, 17)

LE LOUP DEVENU BERGER

Un Loup qui commençoit d'avoir petite part
    Aux Brebis de son voisinage
Crut qu'il faloit s'aider de la peau du Renard
    Et faire un nouveau personnage.
Il s'habille en Berger, endosse un hoqueton,
    Fait sa houlette d'un baston,
    Sans oublier la Cornemuse.
    Pour pousser jusqu'au bout la ruse,
Il auroit volontiers écrit sur son chapeau:
C'est moy qui suis Guillot, Berger de ce troupeau.
    Sa personne estant ainsi faite,
Et ses pieds de devant posez sur sa houlette,
Guillot le sycophante approche doucement.
Guillot le vray Guillot, étendu sur l'herbette,
    Dormoit alors profondément.
Son chien dormoit aussi, comme aussi sa musette.
La pluspart des Brebis dormoient pareillement.
    L'hypocrite les laissa faire,
Et, pour pouvoir mener vers son fort les Brebis,
Il voulut ajoûter la parole aux habits,
    Chose qu'il croyoit necessaire.
    Mais cela gâta son affaire.
Il ne pût du Pasteur contrefaire la voix.
Le ton dont il parla fit retentir les bois,
    Et découvrit tout le mystere.
    Chacun se reveille à ce son,
    Les Brebis, le Chien, le Garçon.
    Le pauvre Loup, dans cet esclandre,
    Empêché par son hoqueton,
    Ne pût ny fuïr ny se défendre.

Toûjours par quelque endroit fourbes se laissent prendre.
    Quiconque est Loup agisse en Loup:
    C'est le plus certain de beaucoup.

THE WOLF TURNED SHEPHERD

A certain wolf there was who, by and by,
    Began to look with jaundiced eye
    Upon his luck: his catch of ewes
    Was growing slimmer day by day.
    Thought he: "I think it's time I play
The fox!" And he reviews the "don'ts," the "dos"
Of fox's feigning craft. Soon will he don
    The shepherd's garb (his rustic smock),
Fashion a staff, tootle a drone... And on
And on he'll forge his fraud. To dupe the flock
Gladly would he have written on his hat:
"Guillot the shepherd![1] Me!" Well, for all that,
With crook betwixt his paws, this sham Guillot
Stealthily creeps apace, *pianissimo*...
Meanwhile Guillot—the real Guillot, that is—
    Lay sleeping on the grass, with his
Sheepdog asleep as well; and, sleeping too,
    His silent pipes... Likewise the sheep—
    Or most of them—lay fast asleep.
    The hypocrite, false through and through,
    Decided what he had to do
To lure the hapless ewe into his lair;
To wit: add human voice to human air.
And so this wolf in shepherd's clothing makes
A vain attempt to speak... The woods around
Roar—not with shepherdly, but wolfly sound!
    What's more, each one at once awakes:
    Sheep, shepherd, dog... And wolf, undone,
    Is set upon by everyone.
Entangled in his smock, our pharisee
    Can neither fend them off nor flee.

Wherefore beware! Frauds, hear my caveat:
Let wolf be wolf; that's what he's ablest at!

(III, 3)

LES GRENOUILLES QUI DEMANDENT UN ROY

Les Grenoüilles, se lassant
De l'estat Democratique,
Par leurs clameurs firent tant
Que Jupin les soûmit au pouvoir Monarchique.
Il leur tomba du Ciel un Roy tout pacifique:
Ce Roy fit toutefois un tel bruit en tombant
Que la gent marécageuse,
Gent fort sotte et fort peureuse,
S'alla cacher sous les eaux,
Dans les joncs, dans les roseaux,
Dans les trous du marécage,
Sans oser de long-temps regarder au visage
Celuy qu'elles croyoient estre un geant nouveau;
Or c'estoit un soliveau,
De qui la gravité fit peur à la premiere
Qui de le voir s'avanturant

THE FROGS WHO ASK FOR A KING

The frogs, in realm aquatic,
Made such a hue and cry—
Grown tired of their condition democratic—
That Jupiter on high,
In gesture duly altruistic,
Bestowed on them a system monarchistic.
In short, a king befell them (literally!),
Out of the sky: calm as could be,
Clearly a pacifistic sort, serene,
But who, in falling, made a noise so harsh,
So loud, that those of swamp persuasion—green,
Timid, and none too bright—hid in the marsh,
Amid the reeds, betwixt, between,
Daring not gaze upon this creature
Whose every feature
Bespoke some fearsome and gigantic being.
He was, in point of fact, a log;

Osa bien quitter sa taniere.
Elle approcha, mais en tremblant.
Une autre la suivit, une autre en fit autant,
Il en vint une fourmilliere;
Et leur troupe à la fin se rendit familiere
Jusqu'à sauter sur l'épaule du Roy.
Le bon Sire le souffre, et se tient toûjours coy.
Jupin en a bien-tost la cervelle rompuë.
Donnez-nous, dit ce peuple, un Roy qui se remuë.
Le Monarque des Dieux leur envoye une Gruë,
Qui les croque, qui les tuë,
Qui les gobe à son plaisir.
Et Grenoüilles de se plaindre;
Et Jupin de leur dire: Et quoy! vostre desir
A ses loix croit-il nous astraindre?
Vous avez dû premierement
Garder vostre Gouvernement;
Mais, ne l'ayant pas fait, il vous devoit suffire
Que vostre premier Roy fust debonnaire et doux:
De celuy-cy contentez-vous,
De peur d'en rencontrer un pire.

A limb, whose weighty air, there in the bog,
Awed the first frog to poke her head; who, seeing
      Our ponderous giant,
   But being a trifle more defiant,
Approached in fear... A second... Then a third...
   And soon the whole marsh-dwelling herd,
    Grown so familiar... Bolder... Bolder...
That there they were, lo! perching on his shoulder!
King Log, compliant, uttered not a word.
At length they prayed to Jupiter; implored,
   Begged, pestered him: "Good god, give us
At least a king that moves!" Olympus' lord,
This time, sends them a crane, who—ravenous—
   Kills, eats, and gulps them down apace.
Race Frog complains. Jupiter answers thus:
"What can I do? Who told you to replace
   The government you had before?
Frankly, you should have kept it! Furthermore,
You got a king as kind as you could get.
   Be happy now with what you've got,
   Wicked though he may be. If not,
The next, mayhap, may be more wicked yet!"

                                 (III, 4)

LE RENARD ET LE BOUC

Capitaine Renard alloit de compagnie
Avec son amy Bouc des plus haut encornez.
Celuy-cy ne voyoit pas plus loin que son nez;
L'autre estoit passé maistre en fait de tromperie.
La soif les obligea de descendre en un puits.
  Là chacun d'eux se desaltere.
Aprés qu'abondamment tous deux en eurent pris,
Le Renard dit au Bouc: Que ferons-nous, compere?
Ce n'est pas tout de boire, il faut sortir d'icy.
Leve tes pieds en haut, et tes cornes aussi:
Mets-les contre le mur. Le long de ton eschine
  Je grimperay premierement;
  Puis sur tes cornes m'élevant,
  A l'aide de cette machine
  De ce lieu-cy je sortiray.
  Aprés quoy je t'en tireray.
—Par ma barbe, dit l'autre, il est bon; et je loüe
  Les gens bien sensez comme toy.
  Je n'aurois jamais, quant à moy,
  Trouvé ce secret, je l'avoue.
Le Renard sort du puits, laisse son compagnon
  Et vous luy fait un beau sermon
  Pour l'exhorter à patience.
Si le Ciel t'eust, dit-il, donné par excellence
Autant de jugement que de barbe au menton,
  Tu n'aurois pas à la legere
Descendu dans ce puits. Or, adieu, j'en suis hors.
Tasche de t'en tirer, et fais tous tes efforts:
  Car, pour moy, j'ay certaine affaire
Qui ne me permet pas d'arrester en chemin.
En toute chose il faut considerer la fin.

THE FOX AND THE GOAT

Renard—that crafty captain, he—
Was going abroad in company
With friend the goat, him of the well-horned head;
    Who, stupid (as is often said),
    Can see no farther than his nose—
Unlike our fox, to humbug born and bred...
    At any rate, the story goes
That one day, parched and dry, the pair descended
    Into a well to quench their thirst.
That done, the question was how they intended
Thence to ascend! Said fox: "Let me go first...
    You, lift your fetlocks high, and lean them
Over against the wall, your head between them:
    I can climb up your back and hoist
    Myself right out, then pull you free."
"Ah, by the blessèd hairs of my goatee!
    Bully!" the goat, impressed, rejoiced.
    "Felicitations! Who but you
    Would think of such a thing! Not I!"
And out climbs fox... then bids his friend adieu.
But not without a sermon, by the by,
    Urging him to be patient. "Why,"
    Says he, "if only heaven had been
As generous with judgment, to your mind,
    As with those whiskers, to your chin,
I daresay you'd have been much less inclined
To jump, without a thought, into that well!
    Well, bye-bye!... Me? I'm leaving now
    On other business. Anyhow,
Keep trying!... And remember, as they tell,
    It's best to look before you leap!"
Quite so. For as we sow, so shall we reap.[1]

(III, 5)

PAROLE DE SOCRATE

Socrate un jour faisant bâtir,
Chacun censuroit son ouvrage.
L'un trouvoit les dedans, pour ne luy point mentir,
Indignes d'un tel personnage;
L'autre blâmoit la face, et tous estoient d'avis
Que les appartemens en estoient trop petits.
Quelle maison pour luy! L'on y tournoit à peine.
Pleust au Ciel que de vrais amis,
Telle qu'elle est, dit-il, elle pût estre pleine!
Le bon Socrate avoit raison
De trouver pour ceux-là trop grande sa maison.
Chacun se dit amy; mais fol qui s'y repose:
Rien n'est plus commun que ce nom,
Rien n'est plus rare que la chose.

A REFLECTION FROM SOCRATES

A house was being built for Socrates.
　　Each passer-by who stops, espies it—
Inside and out—is quick to criticize it.
　　Loudly his loyal devotees
Lament: "For such a man, lodgings like these?
　　Why, one can scarcely turn around!
Such paltry quarters for a man renowned
Round and about!" But Socrates replies:
"Nay, nay! Myself, I pray, contrariwise—
　　Small though they be—that they not be
Even too large for my true friends!" And he
Was right, withal, despite the modest size.
True friends? Though every man pretends to be one,
Rarely, if ever, do we really see one.

(IV, 17)

L'AVARE QUI A PERDU SON TRESOR

L'Usage seulement fait la possession.
Je demande à ces gens de qui la passion
Est d'entasser toûjours, mettre somme sur somme,
Quel avantage ils ont que n'ait pas un autre homme.
Diogene là-bas est aussi riche qu'eux,
Et l'Avare icy haut comme luy vit en gueux.
L'homme au tresor caché qu'Esope nous propose,
    Servira d'exemple à la chose.
      Ce malheureux attendoit
Pour joüir de son bien une seconde vie;
Ne possedoit pas l'or, mais l'or le possedoit.
Il avoit dans la terre une somme enfoüie,
    Son cœur avec, n'ayant autre déduit
      Que d'y ruminer jour et nuit,
Et rendre sa chevance à luy-mesme sacrée.
Qu'il allast ou qu'il vinst, qu'il bust ou qu'il mangeast,
On l'eust pris de bien court, à moins qu'il ne songeast
A l'endroit où gisoit cette somme enterrée.
Il y fit tant de tours qu'un Fossoyeur le vid,
Se douta du dépost, l'enleva sans rien dire.
Nostre Avare un beau jour ne trouva que le nid.
Voilà mon homme aux pleurs; il gemit il soûpire.
    Il se tourmente, il se déchire.
Un passant luy demande à quel sujet ses cris.
    C'est mon tresor que l'on m'a pris.
—Vostre tresor? où pris? —Tout joignant cette pierre.
    —Eh! sommes-nous en temps de guerre
Pour l'apporter si loin? N'eussiez-vous pas mieux fait
De le laisser chez vous en vostre cabinet,
    Que de le changer de demeure?
Vous auriez pû sans peine y puiser à toute heure.
—A toute heure? bons Dieux! Ne tient-il qu'à cela?
    L'argent vient-il comme il s'en va?
Je n'y touchois jamais. —Dites-moy donc de grâce,
Reprit l'autre, pourquoy vous vous affligez tant,
Puisque vous ne touchiez jamais à cet argent:
    Mettez une pierre à la place,
    Elle vous vaudra tout autant.

THE MISER WHO LOST HIS TREASURE

Possessions have no value till we use them.
Misers there are, no doubt, who would dissent.
    This tale, I trust, will disabuse them:
What does it profit them to hold, unspent,
Pile upon pile of gold? Diogenes,
For all his poverty, in death, is quite
As rich; and avarice's devotees
Are quite as poor, in life, as he.[1] Thereto, we might
    Consider one of Æsop's tales: the one
        About a miser and his hoard,
Who wants to wait until his life is done
        (And off he's gone to his reward),
To be reborn before he spends his treasure.[2]
    With it, his heart lies buried; such
That, day and night, he knows no other pleasure
Than to go off and worship it; to touch
The ground; to muse, to dream... Eating or drinking,
Coming or going, one thought ever thinking!
Truly, the gold owns him; not he, the gold.
       Now, in the interim,
A certain graveyard digger, seeing him
       Pay visits to the spot, untold,
Suspects, digs, finds the treasure... And that's that!
Our miser, one fine day, comes, sees the hole—
       Empty, alas!—gazes thereat,
And, heartsick, sighing from his very soul,
Weeps, wails, and groans in grief. A passer-by
       Asks him: "Why all the hue and cry?"
"Why? It's my money! It's been stolen... See?"
       "Oh? Where?" "Next to that rock!" "Dear me,
Are we at war? Why keep it way out here?
You should have kept it in your chiffonier.
       You could have used it when you chose."
       "'Used it?' Good God! Do you suppose
It grows on trees? I never spent a sou."
       "You didn't?" "No!" "Then I suggest
You needn't rend your hair and beat your breast,
       My friend! Here's all you have to do:
That hole of yours... Go take some stones and fill it.
Really, it won't make any difference, will it?
       They'll be worth quite as much to you!"

(IV, 20)

LE RENARD AYANT LA QUEUE COUPEE

Un vieux Renard, mais des plus fins,
Grand croqueur de Poulets, grand preneur de Lapins,
Sentant son Renard d'une lieuë,
Fut enfin au piege attrapé.
Par grand hazard en estant échapé,
Non pas franc, car pour gage il y laissa sa queuë:
S'estant, dis-je, sauvé sans queuë et tout honteux,
Pour avoir des pareils, (comme il estoit habile),
Un jour que les Renards tenoient conseil entr'eux:
Que faisons-nous, dit-il, de ce poids inutile,
Et qui va balayant tous les sentiers fangeux?
Que nous sert cette queuë? Il faut qu'on se la coupe.
Si l'on me croit, chacun s'y resoudra.
—Vostre avis est fort bon, dit quelqu'un de la troupe,
Mais tournez-vous, de grace, et l'on vous répondra.
A ces mots, il se fit une telle huée,
Que le pauvre écourté ne put estre entendu.
Pretendre oster la queuë eust esté temps perdu;
La mode en fut continuée.

THE FOX WHO LOST HIS TAIL

A certain fox, grown old, but nonetheless
Proficient in the ways of foxliness—
Still terror of the henhouse and the hutch,
And smacking of your fox from miles away!—
One day lay trapped. And yet his luck was such
That he escaped; although, to his dismay,
Not quite: that is, he left his tail behind!
And so, thus altered—nay, abbreviated,
Curtailed (if I may say)—humiliated,
     He straightway set about to find
How best he might persuade his fox confreres
     Likewise to rid themselves of theirs.
Next day, in council, boldly he opined:
"Who needs those heavy things we trail in back?
     What good are they, except to track
Through mire and muck! I say we hack them off."
"Do tell!" one of their troop was quick to scoff.
"A fine idea... But first, please turn about."
He does... No use to talk, as all the while
     With hoot and howl, guffaw and shout,
          They drown him out!
     Wherefore, for all our fox's guile,
Yet, truth to tell, the tail is still in style.

                                        (V, 5)

LES MEDECINS

Le Medecin Tant-pis alloit voir un malade,
Que visitoit aussi son confrere Tant-mieux;
Ce dernier esperoit, quoique son camarade
Soûtinst que le gisant iroit voir ses ayeux.
Tous deux s'estant trouvez differens pour la cure,
Leur malade paya le tribut à Nature,
Aprés qu'en ses conseils Tant-pis eust esté crû.
Ils triomphoient encor sur cette maladie.
L'un disoit: Il est mort, je l'avois bien prévû.
—S'il m'eust cru, disoit l'autre, il seroit plein de vie.

THE DOCTORS

A patient in the sickest of conditions
Was visited by each of his physicians:
Hopeless and Hopeful, doctors twain. The second
Thought he could save him, though the first one reckoned
Nature would claim her due; his regimen
Prevailed, and that was that. Whereat, amen!…
Yet, even though their patient died, each boasted.
Said Hopeless: "Dead! I told you so! You see?"
And Hopeful, no less satisfied, riposted:
"He'd still be living if they'd heeded me!"

(V, 12)

LE CERF ET LA VIGNE

Un Cerf, à la faveur d'une Vigne fort haute
Et telle qu'on en voit en de certains climats,
S'estant mis à couvert et sauvé du trépas,
Les Veneurs pour ce coup croyoient leurs chiens en faute.
Ils les rappellent donc. Le Cerf hors de danger
Broute sa bienfaitrice, ingratitude extrême!
On l'entend, on retourne, on le fait déloger,
      Il vient mourir en ce lieu mesme.
J'ay merité, dit-il, ce juste chastiment:
Profitez-en, ingrats. Il tombe en ce moment.
La Meute en fait curée. Il luy fut inutile
De pleurer aux Veneurs à sa mort arrivez.
Vraye image de ceux qui profanent l'azile
      Qui les a conservez.

THE DEER AND THE VINE

A deer pursued by hounds had found some high,
　　Thick vines—the kind we find betimes
　　Growing in certain other climes—
And, hiding in them, saved his skin thereby.
The hunters think their dogs have failed to track
Their prey, and promptly call them off. The deer,
Now out of danger from the murderous pack—
Lacking in proper gratitude, alack!—
Bites at his savior... Chomps... The huntsmen hear,
Turn round, come back, and flush him out. Soon will
He die, there, where he stands. "Alas," sighs he,
"I earn my doom! Ungrateful souls, see me
　　And learn." With that, in for the kill,
　　The hounds, with fang and claw, gouge, gore him.
Deaf to his tears, the hunters quite ignore him.
Such is the fate of those whose desecration
Sullies the refuge that was their salvation.

(V, 15)

LE SERPENT ET LA LIME

On conte qu'un serpent voisin d'un Horloger
(C'estoit pour l'Horloger un mauvais voisinage)
Entra dans sa boutique, et cherchant à manger
    N'y rencontra pour tout potage
Qu'une Lime d'acier qu'il se mit à ronger.
Cette Lime luy dit, sans se mettre en colere:
    Pauvre ignorant! et que pretends-tu faire?
      Tu te prends à plus dur que toy.
      Petit Serpent à teste folle,
      Plutost que d'emporter de moy
      Seulement le quart d'une obole,
      Tu te romprois toutes les dents.
      Je ne crains que celles du temps.

Cecy s'adresse à vous, esprits du dernier ordre,
Qui n'estant bons à rien cherchez sur tout à mordre.
    Vous vous tourmentez vainement.
Croyez-vous que vos dents impriment leurs outrages
      Sur tant de beaux ouvrages?
Ils sont pour vous d'airain, d'acier, de diamant.

THE SNAKE AND THE FILE

They tell about a snake who made his nest
Next to a clocksmith's shop—not quite the best
Of company the clocksmith might have kept!—[1]
And who crept in one day in search of food;
Found nothing, not a crumb; nothing except
A metal file, on which he promptly chewed.
    "Poor fool, what do you think you're doing?"
Calmly the file inquired. "Poor silly snake!
I'm hard, you're soft. What makes you think you'll make
    Even a dent with all your chewing?
You'll break your teeth and never even harm me:
    None but the teeth of Time alarm me."

This fable is for you, my fine *messieurs*
Of little talent, who, with biting slur
Attack at every turn. Your brash harangues—
        Your critic-fangs—
Do nothing to the works you spurn. In vain
You gnash and gnaw. For it will come to pass
That, unlike yours, those works will long remain:
Solid as diamond, tough as steel and brass.

(v, 16)

LE LION S'EN ALLANT EN GUERRE

Le Lion dans sa teste avoit une entreprise.
Il tint conseil de guerre, envoya ses Prevosts,
     Fit avertir les animaux:
Tous furent du dessein, chacun selon sa guise.
     L'Elephant devoit sur son dos
     Porter l'attirail necessaire
     Et combattre à son ordinaire,
     L'Ours s'apprester pour les assauts,
Le Renard ménager de secrettes pratiques,
Et le Singe amuser l'ennemi par ses tours.
Renvoyez, dit quelqu'un, les Asnes qui sont lourds,
Et les Liévres sujets à des terreurs paniques.
—Point du tout, dit le Roy, je les veux employer.
Nostre troupe sans eux ne seroit pas complete.
L'Asne effrayra les gens, nous servant de trompete,
Et le Liévre pourra nous servir de courrier.

     Le Monarque prudent et sage
De ses moindres sujets sçait tirer quelque usage,
     Et connoist les divers talens:
Il n'est rien d'inutile aux personnes de sens.

THE LION GOING OFF TO WAR

The lion, bent on action military,
Convoked his council for deliberation
   In session extraordinary,
   Then sent his marshals through the nation
   To tell his subjects of his plan.
Each one, unto a man (or beast, that is),
Agrees to use his gifts as best he can:
   The elephant, that back of his
To carry the equipment, and his strength,
To launch the first attack; the bear, at length,
   To lay the siege; the fox, to act
With subterfuge; the monkey, to distract
With tricks... Then someone says: "The ass and rabbit[1]
Have no good use; best send them home. The one
   Is nothing but a simpleton;
   The other has the nasty habit
Of turning tail in fright!" Says lion: "Nay!
The ass can be our trumpet. With his bray
   He'll terrify the enemy; whereas
   The rabbit, with that speed he has,
Can be our courier."

        Wise the king, to have refused.
Even the least have skills: let them be used!

                        (V, 19)

L'OURS ET LES DEUX COMPAGNONS

Deux compagnons pressez d'argent
A leur voisin Fourreur vendirent
La peau d'un Ours encor vivant,
Mais qu'ils tuëroient bien-tost, du moins à ce qu'ils dirent.
C'estoit le Roy des Ours au compte de ces gens.
Le Marchand à sa peau devoit faire fortune.
Elle garentiroit des froids les plus cuisans.
On en pourroit fourrer plutost deux robes qu'une.
Dindenaut prisoit moins ses Moutons qu'eux leur Ours:
Leur, à leur compte, et non à celuy de la Beste.
S'offrant de la livrer au plus tard dans deux jours,
Ils conviennent de prix, et se mettent en queste,
Trouvent l'Ours qui s'avance, et vient vers eux au trot.
Voilà mes gens frappez comme d'un coup de foudre.
Le marché ne tint pas; il falut le resoudre:
D'interests contre l'Ours, on n'en dit pas un mot.
L'un des deux Compagnons grimpe au faiste d'un arbre;

THE BEAR AND THE TWO COMPANIONS

Two churls—an impecunious pair—
    Went to a furrier to persuade him
That they were sure to slay a certain bear
(The king of bears, in fact!); that once they'd flayed him,
He would do well to have the skin. "We swear,
    You'll reap a fortune from it! Why,
Fur enough is there in it to defy
    The bitter chill; enough to line
Not one but two fine cloaks of your design!"
Not even Dindonneau, who prized his sheep,[1]
Will sing their praise with an affection half as deep
    As do they for "our bear," "our skin." For "theirs"
        It is already, not the bear's!
So, promising to bring it round next day
Or two, they haggle, hit upon a sum:
"Agreed!" And off they go to fetch their prey—
    As yet uncaught, but anyway…
    Indeed, they find him; see him come
Loping headlong to meet them! Now, struck dumb,

L'autre plus froid que n'est un marbre,
Se couche sur le nez, fait le mort, tient son vent,
        Ayant quelque part oüy dire
        Que l'Ours s'acharne peu souvent
Sur un corps qui ne vit, ne meut, ny ne respire.
Seigneur Ours, comme un sot, donna dans ce panneau.
Il void ce corps gisant, le croit privé de vie,
        Et de peur de supercherie
Le tourne, le retourne, approche son museau,
        Flaire aux passages de l'haleine.
C'est, dit-il, un cadavre; Ostons-nous, car il sent.
A ces mots, l'Ours s'en va dans la forest prochaine.
L'un de nos deux Marchands de son arbre descend,
Court à son compagnon, luy dit que c'est merveille
Qu'il n'ait eu seulement que la peur pour tout mal.
Et bien, ajoûta-t-il, la peau de l'animal?
        Mais que t'a-t-il dit à l'oreille?
        Car il s'approchoit de bien prés,
        Te retournant avec sa serre.
        —Il m'a dit qu'il ne faut jamais
Vendre la peau de l'Ours qu'on ne l'ait mis par terre.

They lose all thoughts commercial, peer around,
Think only how to save *their* skin from *him*!
One climbs a tree, up to the topmost limb;
The other, numb with fright, nose to the ground,
Lies down, quick as a wink; makes not a rustle;
    Breathes not a breath; moves not a muscle.
    For somewhere he has heard it said
That bears will not attack those lying thus…
Well, Seigneur Bear, properly credulous,
Is fooled: he sees a body, thinks it's dead.
Still, to be sure, he comes and, with his muzzle,
    Sniffs at the nose, gives it a nuzzle.
    "Yes," he decides, "it's dead, methinks.
    It must be, seeing how much it stinks…"
And off he goes. Our huckster up the tree
Comes down, runs over, greets his friend with glee,
Happy to see he's none the worse for fear,
    Saying: "Well now, when do we skin it?…
And what was that he whispered in your ear,
Pawing your head?" The other: "Ha!…'Compeer,'
He said, 'don't sell the bearskin with the bear still in it!'"[2]

(V, 20)

L'ASNE VESTU DE LA PEAU DU LION

De la peau du Lion l'Asne s'étant vestu
    Estoit craint par tout à la ronde,
    Et bien qu'animal sans vertu,
    Il faisoit trembler tout le monde.
Un petit bout d'oreille échapé par malheur
    Découvrit la fourbe et l'erreur.
    Martin fit alors son office.
Ceux qui ne sçavoient pas la ruse et la malice
    S'estonnoient de voir que Martin
    Chassast les Lions au moulin.

    Force gens font du bruit en France
Par qui cet Apologue est rendu familier.
    Un équipage cavalier
    Fait les trois quarts de leur vaillance.

THE ASS DRESSED IN THE LION'S SKIN

An ass, dressed in a lion's skin—
Though quite the worthless beast—in so dissembling,
Terrified all who saw him decked therein
And filled the woods about with fear and trembling.
    But soon—ah woe!—a bit of ear
    (His own, I mean) chanced to appear
    From under his untoward disguise: it
Gave him away; Martin the miller spies it,[1]
And, quick to realize it's all a trick,
    Puts him to work, turning the mill.
Amazed are those, thinking him lion still,
Who marvel that Martin, with but his stick,
Can bend a lion to a miller's will!

    Many in France today are able
    To prove the wisdom of this fable:
Seeing their jaunty garb we gaze, impressed;[2]
    But little are they, or less, undressed!

(V, 21)

LE RENARD, LE SINGE, ET LES ANIMAUX

Les Animaux, au deceds d'un Lion,
En son vivant Prince de la contrée,
Pour faire un Roy s'assemblerent, dit-on.
De son étuy la couronne est tirée.
Dans une chartre un Dragon la gardoit.
Il se trouva que sur tous essayée
A pas un d'eux elle ne convenoit.
Plusieurs avoient la teste trop menuë,
Aucuns trop grosse, aucuns mesme cornuë.
Le Singe aussi fit l'épreuve en riant,
Et par plaisir la Tiare essayant,
Il fit autour force grimaceries,
Tours de souplesse, et mille singeries,
Passa dedans ainsi qu'en un cerceau.
Aux Animaux cela sembla si beau
Qu'il fut élû: chacun luy fit hommage.
Le Renard seul regreta son suffrage,

THE FOX, THE APE, AND THE ANIMALS

A lion, monarch of the country round,
Had reigned throughout his life. In time, he died.
The animals assembled to decide
Which one amongst them should be duly crowned.
The Keeper of the Royal Diadem—
A dungeon dragon—brought it forth. Each one
In turn tried the tiara on, but none—
Not one—could make it fit. For some of them
It was too large (those small of head); for some,
Too small (conversely, large); some too there were
With horns!... In sum, no one in creaturedom
Succeeded. That is, not until *monsieur*
The ape tried too, just for the fun of it...
He tugs, contorts, screws up his face... The clown
Performs such monkey mischief with the crown
That, in the end, behold! A perfect fit!
Impressed, the beasts elect him, pay their court,
Honor him with respect, with genuflexion...

Sans toutefois montrer son sentiment.
Quand il eut fait son petit compliment,
Il dit au Roy: Je sçay, Sire, une cache,
Et ne crois pas qu'autre que moy la sçache.
Or tout tresor par droit de Royauté
Appartient, Sire, à vôtre Majesté.
Le nouveau Roy baaille aprés la Finance,
Luy-même y court pour n'estre pas trompé.
C'estoit un piége: il y fut attrapé.
Le Renard dit au nom de l'assistance:
Pretendrois-tu nous gouverner encor,
Ne sçachant pas te conduire toy-même?
Il fut démis; et l'on tomba d'accord
Qu'à peu de gens convient le Diadême.

Only the fox, a rather cynical sort,
Regrets the consequence of their selection.
Hiding his feelings, though, he comes before
His Highness, says two flattering words—no more—
Then: "Sire, there is a treasure trove close by.
By royal right it's yours. But only I
And I alone know where it is." He tells him...
King Ape's cupidity for wealth compels him
Thither to fly, to see with his own eye...
Alas, it was a trap, and he got caught!
Whereat the fox was pleased to share his thought.
Said he: "How can you govern us when you
Govern yourself so ill?" Without ado,
Thereat was ape dethroned, undone, brought down,
As all agreed that few—yes, very few—
Truly deserve, indeed, to wear a crown.

(VI, 6)

LE MULET SE VANTANT DE SA GENEALOGIE

Le Mulet d'un Prelat se piquoit de noblesse,
    Et ne parloit incessamment
    Que de sa mere la Jument,
    Dont il contoit mainte proüesse.
Elle avoit fait cecy, puis avoit esté là.
    Son fils prétendoit, pour cela,
    Qu'on le dust mettre dans l'Histoire.
Il eust cru s'abaisser servant un Medecin.
Estant devenu vieux, on le mit au moulin.
Son pere l'Asne alors luy revint en memoire.

    Quand le malheur ne seroit bon
    Qu'à mettre un sot à la raison;
    Toûjours seroit-ce à juste cause
    Qu'on le dit bon à quelque chose.

After Goya

THE MULE WHO BOASTED OF HIS FAMILY TREE

A priest there was who owned a mule. The latter,
   Proud of his pedigree, would natter
   Endlessly on, *extempore,*
About his genteel mother-mare, and bray
Her noble exploits—here, there, everywhere.
Wherefore said offspring felt that History—
   So ancient was her family tree—
Owed him a place; felt, with his high-born air,
That it would be beneath his dignity
Even to serve a doctor, say... Alas,
In time our mule grew old, and straightway he was hauled
   Off to the mill, where, straightway, he recalled
His father, who had been a low-born ass.

   If woe had but one use—to wit,
   To chasten fools (as well it should)—
   Yet could we rightly say of it:
   "Ill is the wind that blows no good."

(VI, 7)

LE VIEILLARD ET L'ASNE

Un Vieillard sur son Asne apperçut en passant
    Un Pré plein d'herbe et fleurissant.
Il y lâche sa beste, et le Grison se ruë
    Au travers de l'herbe menuë,
    Se veautrant, gratant, et frotant,
    Gambadant, chantant et broutant,
    Et faisant mainte place nette.
    L'ennemi vient sur l'entrefaite:
    Fuyons, dit alors le Vieillard.
    —Pourquoy? répondit le paillard.
Me fera-t-on porter double bast, double charge?
—Non pas, dit le Vieillard, qui prit d'abord le large.
—Et que m'importe donc, dit l'Asne, à qui je sois?
    Sauvez-vous, et me laissez paistre:
    Nôtre ennemy, c'est nôtre Maistre:
    Je vous le dis en bon François.

THE OLD MAN AND THE ASS

An old man had an ass. Astride it,
Passing a grassy field, he stops beside it,
   Looses the beast to let it graze.
Thereat the latter frisks and frolics, brays,
Pads through the flowers, the shrubs, scratching and pawing,
   Gamboling joyously, hee-hawing…
Suddenly though—ah woe!—a brigand shows
   His face! Alarmed, the old man goes
To flee; calls to the jackass: "Come, let's fly!"
"Oh? Will he make me carry twice the load?"
   "No," shouts the master, down the road,
   Well on his way. "Then tell me why.
   What difference can it make to me
Whose load I bear? So humbug!" he tut-tuts.
   "Go! You run off and let me be.
Every master is my enemy!
   Plain talk: no ifs, no ands, no buts."[1]

(VI, 8)

LE LIEVRE ET LA TORTUE

Rien ne sert de courir; il faut partir à point.
Le Lievre et la Tortuë en sont un témoignage.
Gageons, dit celle-cy, que vous n'atteindrez point
Si-tost que moy ce but. — Si-tost? Estes-vous sage?
    Repartit l'animal leger.
    Ma commere, il vous faut purger
    Avec quatre grains d'ellebore.
    — Sage ou non, je parie encore.
    Ainsi fut fait: et de tous deux
    On mit prés du but les enjeux.
    Sçavoir quoy, ce n'est pas l'affaire,
    Ni de quel juge l'on convint.
Nostre Lievre n'avoit que quatre pas à faire;
J'entends de ceux qu'il fait lorsque prest d'estre atteint
Il s'éloigne des chiens, les renvoye aux Calendes
    Et leur fait arpenter les Landes.
Ayant, dis-je, du temps de reste pour brouter,
    Pour dormir, et pour écouter
   D'où vient le vent, il laisse la Tortuë

THE HARE AND THE TORTOISE

To win the race you needn't run; just start on time.
    Witness the subjects of my rhyme
    Herewith: the tortoise and the hare.
"I'll bet," proposed the former to the latter,
"That I can beat you, going from here to there."
Thinking her daft, the hare looked squarely at her.
    "My dear," he asked, "are you quite sane?"
Perhaps an enema would clear your brain…
    Four grains of hellebore should do it."
"Sane or insane," said she, "come, let's go to it!"
So be it. And the bets are placed. How much
    The stakes? Indeed, no matter, nor
Who is the judge they choose to race before…
Hare would have found four hops sufficient: such
    As those he makes when, in the nick
Of time—chased, almost caught, bounding away—
He leaves the hound to stalk his baliwick,
Promising to come play "some other day!"
    Now, as I say, the cunning hare
    Knows he has time enough to spare:
    "Why bother to start running yet?

Aller son train de Senateur.
Elle part, elle s'évertuë;
Elle se haste avec lenteur.
Luy cependant méprise une telle victoire,
Tient la gageure à peu de gloire,
Croit qu'il y va de son honneur
De partir tard. Il broute, il se repose,
Il s'amuse à toute autre chose
Qu'à la gageure. A la fin quand il vid
Que l'autre touchoit presque au bout de la carriere,
Il partit comme un trait; mais les élans qu'il fit
Furent vains: la Tortuë arriva la premiere.
Hé bien! luy cria-t-elle, avois-je pas raison?
Dequoy vous sert vostre vîtesse?
Moy, l'emporter! Et que seroit-ce
Si vous portiez une maison?

I'll wait a bit… Browse… Maybe get
My forty winks… See how the wind is blowing…"
　　As for the tortoise, she gets going,
　　Creeps graybeard-like, makes her slow haste…
　　The hare, meanwhile—with much distaste
And scorn for such an easy victory—
Feels that his honor quite demands that he
Wait longer to begin. He browses, rests,
Passes the time with other interests
More pleasing than their wager… Finally,
He spies the tortoise… Look! She's almost at
The point proposed!… Off like a dart he flies…
Bounds… Leaps… But no! In vain: she beats him flat!
　　"Well, well! Indeed! Me? Win?" she cries.
　　"What good did all your speed do you?
　　　　So, was I right or wrong?
Then too, I have to ask what you would do
If you were forced to drag your house along!"

(VI, 10)

L'ASNE ET SES MAISTRES

L'Asne d'un Jardinier se plaignoit au destin
De ce qu'on le faisoit lever devant l'Aurore.
Les Coqs, luy disoit-il, ont beau chanter matin;
    Je suis plus matineux encore.
Et pourquoy? Pour porter des herbes au marché.
Belle necessité d'interrompre mon somme!
    Le Sort de sa plainte touché
Luy donne un autre Maistre; et l'Animal de somme
Passe du Jardinier aux mains d'un Corroyeur.
La pesanteur des peaux, et leur mauvaise odeur
Eurent bien-tost choqué l'impertinente Beste.
J'ay regret, disoit-il, à mon premier Seigneur.
    Encor quand il tournoit la teste,
    J'attrapois, s'il m'en souvient bien,
Quelque morceau de chou qui ne me coutoit rien.
Mais icy, point d'aubeine; ou si j'en ay quelqu'une,
C'est de coups. Il obtint changement de fortune,
    Et sur l'état d'un Charbonnier
    Il fut couché tout le dernier.
Autre plainte. Quoy donc! dit le Sort en colere,
    Ce Baudet-cy m'occupe autant
    Que cent Monarques pourroient faire.
Croit-il estre le seul qui ne soit pas content?
    N'ay-je en l'esprit que son affaire?

Le Sort avoit raison; tous gens sont ainsi faits:
Nostre condition jamais ne nous contente:
    La pire est toujours la presente.
Nous fatiguons le Ciel à force de placets.
Qu'à chacun Jupiter accorde sa requeste,
    Nous luy romprons encor la teste.

THE ASS AND HIS MASTERS

The gardener's ass complained to Fate that he
Was made to rise before the dawn each day.
"Let the cocks fuss," he grumbled bitterly,
    "That they must crow at sun's first ray.
    Me? I rise earlier still than they!
And why? To lug my load of hay and straw
    Off to the blessèd marketplace.
What? Interrupt my sleep for that? Hee-haw
      And pshaw! It's a disgrace!"
Fate, moved by his lament, changes the ass's
    Master: the brazen pack-beast passes
Into a tanner's hands...[1] But soon the fetid
Stench and the heavy hides he has to haul
    Appall, repel him. "All in all,
    I should have kept the first," he fretted.
"Each time he turned his head I sneaked a bite—
Cabbage, whatever... Now? Alas, not quite!
From this one I get nothing, only blows!"
Fate listened: once again, touched by his woes,
She made the change... Now, long into the night,
He labors for a coalman, never ceasing;
Complains again... Poor Fate, complaining too,
    Cries: "Really, now!" her wrath increasing.
    "This jackass gives me more to do
Than any hundred kings! The world's a-crawl
With malcontents. Does he suppose withal
That I have none but him to cater to?"

Fate knew whereof she spoke. We, one and all,
    Loathe our condition; curse, decry it;
    Pray to the heavens to rectify it.
Jove and his gods relent? Still we indict 'em;
Hound him with our lament, *ad infinitum*.[2]

(VI, 11)

LE VILLAGEOIS ET LE SERPENT

Esope conte qu'un Manant
Charitable autant que peu sage,
Un jour d'Hyver se promenant
A l'entour de son heritage,
Apperçut un Serpent sur la neige étendu,
Transi, gelé, perclus, immobile rendu,
N'ayant pas à vivre un quart d'heure.
Le Villageois le prend, l'emporte en sa demeure,
Et sans considerer quel sera le loyer
D'une action de ce merite,
Il l'étend le long du foyer,
Le réchauffe, le ressuscite.
L'Animal engourdi sent à peine le chaud,
Que l'ame luy revient avecque la colere.
Il leve un peu la teste, et puis siffle aussi-tost,
Puis fait un long repli, puis tâche à faire un saut

THE PEASANT AND THE SNAKE

Æsop it was who told about
A none-too-clever village lout—
But kind of heart—who, as he strolled
Without his habitat, one bitter cold
And wintry day, discovered, lo!
There, lying all but lifeless on the snow,
Chilled through and through, frozen quite stiff, a snake.
The rustic, touched, made up his mind to take
The poor beast home, with no suspicion
Just how his altruistic disposition
Would be repaid. He laid him down close by him,
Next to the fire, to warm, revivify him…
No sooner has the beast come thawing back
To life than there he is, poised to attack:
Head raised a bit… a-coil… a-hiss…

Contre son bienfaiteur, son sauveur et son pere.
Ingrat, dit le Manant, voilà donc mon salaire?
Tu mourras. A ces mots, plein d'un juste courroux,
Il vous prend sa cognée, il vous tranche la Beste,
  Il fait trois Serpens de deux coups,
  Un tronçon, la queuë, et la teste.
L'insecte sautillant cherche à se réunir,
  Mais il ne put y parvenir.

  Il est bon d'estre charitable;
  Mais envers qui, c'est là le poinct.
  Quant aux ingrats, il n'en est point
  Qui ne meure enfin miserable.

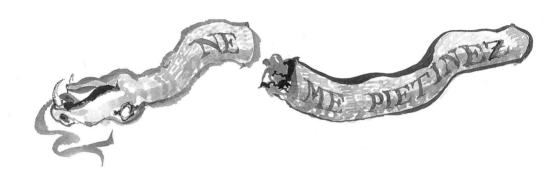

73

Ready to strike the savior who
With care paternal succored him. "What's this?"
The latter cries. "What kind of wretch are you?"
Is that your gratitude? Well then, you're dead!"
    So saying, he takes his trusty axe
And, filled with righteous wrath, with two sharp hacks
Makes three snakes out of one: tail, middle, head.
The trio wants to form anew...[1] It tries...
In vain: it quivers, twitches... promptly dies.

Charity is a virtue, but toward whom?
    Best choose the ones you show it to!
As for ungrateful cads, none are there who,
Sooner or later, fail to meet their doom.

(VI, 13)

LE LION MALADE ET LE RENARD

De par le Roy des Animaux,
Qui dans son antre estoit malade,
Fut fait sçavoir à ses vassaux
Que chaque espece en ambassade
Envoyast gens le visiter,
Sous promesse de bien traiter
Les Deputez, eux et leur suite,
Foy de Lion tres-bien écrite.
Bon passe-port contre la dent;
Contre la griffe tout autant.
L'Edit du Prince s'execute.
De chaque espace on luy députe.

THE SICK LION AND THE FOX

The king of beasts, who, in his lair
Lay ill, had it sent forth forthwith,
To all his vassals everywhere,
Of every stripe, that they prepare
To send some of their kin and kith—
Ambassador, ambassadress—
To visit him in his distress,
Promising—lion's honor!—that
No harm would come to them thereat
Or to their retinue, and plighting
Therefor to put his word in writing:
Passport against his tooth and claw.
His Majesty's word being the law,
The edict goes abroad, inviting

Les Renards gardant la maison,
Un d'eux en dit cette raison:
Les pas empreints sur la poussiere
Par ceux qui s'en vont faire au malade leur cour,
Tous, sans exception, regardent sa taniere;
Pas un ne marque de retour.
Cela nous met en méfiance.
Que sa Majesté nous dispense.
Grammercy de son passe-port.
Je le crois bon; mais dans cet antre
Je vois fort bien comme l'on entre,
Et ne vois pas comme on en sort.

Delegates from each race... They come:
All but the foxes, who for some
Good reason spurn the invitation.
"After all due deliberation,"
One of them says, "we dare not do it.
Many have gone to visit: many's the track
Before our monarch's lair. But, as we view it,
All of them lead directly to it;
None, on the other hand, leads back.
We thank him for his passport—good, no doubt—
But pray we be excused. As for his den,
It's clear how one goes in, but then
Not clear at all how one comes out."

(VI, 14)

LE CHEVAL ET L'ASNE

En ce monde il se faut l'un l'autre secourir.
    Si ton voisin vient à mourir,
    C'est sur toy que le fardeau tombe.

Un Asne accompagnoit un Cheval peu courtois,
Celuy-cy ne portant que son simple harnois,
Et le pauvre Baudet si chargé qu'il succombe.
Il pria le Cheval de l'aider quelque peu:
Autrement il mourroit devant qu'estre à la ville.
La priere, dit-il, n'en est pas incivile:
Moitié de ce fardeau ne vous sera que jeu.
Le Cheval refusa, fit une petarrade:
Tant qu'il vid sous le faix mourir son camarade,
    Et reconnut qu'il avoit tort.
    Du Baudet, en cette avanture,
    On luy fit porter la voiture,
    Et la peau par dessus encor.

THE HORSE AND THE ASS

In this world one must help one's brothers.
Your neighbor dies? Alas, his load
Falls on your shoulders, not another's.

A selfish horse was trotting down the road,
With, by his side, an ass, a-clitter-clatter.
The former beast bore nothing on his back
Save a light harness; whereas, for the latter—
Dragging his cart, trudging beneath his pack—
    It was a very different matter...
"Please, can you help?" the ass politely pled.
    "Ever so little, friend, I pray?
If not, before we reach the town, I'm dead!
For you, why, half my load would be mere play!"
Snob steed farts his reply... The ass, denied,
    Indeed, as he predicted, died.
"Ah me, how wrong I was," then sighed the horse.
    For now our ass's load, perforce,
Was his: cart, pack, and even—truth to tell—
    The ass's skin and bones as well.

(VI, 16)

LES ANIMAUX MALADES DE LA PESTE

Un mal qui répand la terreur,
Mal que le Ciel en sa fureur
Inventa pour punir les crimes de la terre,
La Peste (puis qu'il faut l'appeller par son nom),
Capable d'enrichir en un jour l'Acheron,
Faisoit aux animaux la guerre.
Ils ne mouroient pas tous, mais tous estoient frappez.
On n'en voyoit point d'occupez
A chercher le soûtien d'une mourante vie;
Nul mets n'excitoit leur envie.
Ni Loups ni Renards n'épioient
La douce et l'innocente proye.
Les Tourterelles se fuyoient;
Plus d'amour, partant plus de joye.
Le Lion tint conseil, et dit: Mes chers amis,
Je crois que le Ciel a permis
Pour nos pechez cette infortune;
Que le plus coupable de nous
Se sacrifie aux traits du celeste courroux;
Peut-estre il obtiendra la guerison commune.
L'histoire nous apprend qu'en de tels accidens
On fait de pareils dévoûmens.
Ne nous flatons donc point, voyons sans indulgence
L'état de nostre conscience.
Pour moy, satisfaisant mes appetits gloutons,
J'ay devoré force moutons.
Que m'avoient-ils fait? Nulle offense.
Mesme il m'est arrivé quelquefois de manger
Le Berger.
Je me dévoûray donc, s'il le faut; mais je pense
Qu'il est bon que chacun s'accuse ainsi que moy:
Car on doit souhaiter selon toute justice
Que le plus coupable perisse.
—Sire, dit le Renard, vous estes trop bon Roy;
Vos scrupules font voir trop de delicatesse;
Et bien, manger moutons, canaille, sotte espece,
Est-ce un peché? Non, non: Vous leur fistes, Seigneur,
En les croquant beaucoup d'honneur.
Et quant au Berger, l'on peut dire
Qu'il estoit digne de tous maux,
Estant de ces gens-là qui sur les animaux
Se font un chimerique empire.

THE ANIMALS ILL WITH THE PLAGUE

Long years ago a blight attacked
The world: a blight whose very name gives cause
    For fear and trembling; one that was
Invented by the gods and sent, in fact,
As punishment. The Plague—for why should one
    Not call it by its name?—waged war
Upon the beasts. Each day saw more and more
Enrich the waters of the Acheron.[1]
Some lived, but all were touched. And even they
    Who somehow managed to survive
    Found little life in being alive:
No appetite could whet their palates... Nay,
Foxes and wolves shunned young and tender prey;
    Turtledoves spurned their mates: no love,
No joy was there, nor any hope thereof...
The lion, thereupon, held council. "Friends,"
Said he, "it's clear, I fear, that heaven above
    Repays our sins. To make amends
    And cleanse us of this scourge, the worst
Sinner amongst us must, in sacrifice,
Be offered to the gods. That is the price
Their wrath demands. Indeed, past ages cursed
With such disaster did as much. Let us
Confess our wrongs with candor; me, the first:
    Myself, the vicious, gluttonous,
    Rapacious creature that I am!
    How many a blameless sheep and lamb
    Did I devour! And for what crime?
No crime at all! What's more, from time to time,
I ate my share—as I am wont to do—
        Of shepherd too!
Yes, sacrifice myself I will; though best,
    Perhaps, I wait until the rest
Of you confess as I have done, lest we
    Not put to death the guiltiest."
To which the fox replies: "Your Majesty,
    Your charity and thoughtfulness
Are much to be admired. Nevertheless,
You err. So, you ate sheep? What sin is that?
Vile beasts! Your royal jaws exalted them!
As for the shepherd... Well, it's tit for tat.
    I dare assert, *ad hominem,*
    That he—one of that misbegot

Ainsi dit le Renard, et flateurs d'applaudir.
      On n'osa trop approfondir
Du Tigre, ni de l'Ours, ni des autres puissances
      Les moins pardonnables offenses.
Tous les gens querelleurs, jusqu'aux simples mastins,
Au dire de chacun estoient de petits saints.
L'Asne vint à son tour et dit: J'ay souvenance
      Qu'en un pré de Moines passant,
La faim, l'occasion, l'herbe tendre, et, je pense,
      Quelque diable aussi me poussant,
Je tondis de ce pré la largeur de ma langue.
Je n'en avois nul droit, puis qu'il faut parler net.
A ces mots on cria haro sur le baudet.
Un Loup quelque peu clerc prouva par sa harangue
Qu'il faloit dévoüer ce maudit animal,
Ce pelé, ce galeux, d'où venoit tout leur mal.
Sa peccadille fut jugée un cas pendable.
Manger l'herbe d'autruy! quel crime abominable!
      Rien que la mort n'estoit capable
D'expier son forfait: on le luy fit bien voir.
Selon que vous serez puissant ou miserable,
Les jugemens de Cour vous rendront blanc ou noir.

And evil race that thinks it can
 Subject us all, the race of Man—
Got what was due him and deserved his lot."
So spoke the fox, to many a loud huzzah
 And sycophantic "oh" and "ah"…
As for the tiger's and the bear's confessions—
Others' as well, of fierce and fearsome breed,
Down to the lowest mastiff—none paid heed
To their outrageous, heinous, foul transgressions.
 Rather it was by all agreed
That they were saintly souls!… The ass, at last,
 Appeared. "I must confess," said he,
 "That one day as I trotted past
A cloister green, some devil tempted me
(My hunger too, and opportunity!),
And I went nibbling through a swath of grass:
 A tongue's width, little more, but still…"
Ah! When they heard him, cries of "Kill him! Kill…"
Rang out against our scurvy, ragtag ass.
Whereat, a slightly lettered wolf it was
Who, heaping evidence aplenty on them,
Citing them chapter, codicil, and clause
("To eat another's grass! Are there no laws?"),
 Proved that his sin had brought this plague upon them!
Well, die he must! Our courtiers judge us black or white:
Moral? The weak are always wrong; the strong are right.

(VII, 1)

LES VAUTOURS ET LES PIGEONS

Mars autrefois mit tout l'air en émûte.
Certain sujet fit naistre la dispute
Chez les oiseaux: non ceux que le Printemps
Meine à sa Cour, et qui sous la feüillée
Par leur exemple et leurs sons éclatans,
Font que Venus est en nous réveillée;
Ny ceux encor que la Mere d'Amour
Met à son char; mais le peuple Vautour,
Au bec retors, à la tranchante serre,
Pour un chien mort se fit, dit-on, la guerre.
Il plut du sang; je n'exagere point.
Si je voulois conter de poinct en poinct

THE VULTURES AND THE PIGEONS

Mars once—back when the world was young—
Caused quite a stir on high, among
The birds: great hue and cry arose
Throughout a certain race thereof.
No, not the chirping breed; not those
Spring brings to court to sing of love
In leafy bower, and rouse in us
Venus's image amorous;
Nor those whom she—young Cupid's mother
Yokes to her chariot.[1] Nay, another
People indeed: the vultures! They
Of piercing claw and sharp-hooked bill
Warred with each other. (People say
For some dead dog! Well anyway...)

Tout le détail, je manquerois d'haleine.
Maint chef perit, maint heros expira;
Et sur son roc Prométhée espera
De voir bien-tost une fin à sa peine.
C'estoit plaisir d'observer leurs efforts;
C'estoit pitié de voir tomber les morts.
Valeur, adresse, et ruses, et surprises,
Tout s'employa. Les deux troupes éprises
D'ardent courroux n'épargnoient nuls moyens
De peupler l'air que respirent les ombres:
Tout element remplit de citoyens
Le vaste enclos qu'ont les royaumes sombres.
Cette fureur mit la compassion
Dans les esprits d'une autre nation
Au col changeant, au cœur tendre et fidéle.
Elle employa sa mediation
Pour accorder une telle querelle.
Ambassadeurs par le peuple Pigeon
Furent choisis, et si bien travaillerent,
Que les Vautours plus ne se chamaillerent.
Ils firent treve, et la paix s'ensuivit.
Helas! ce fut aux dépens de la race
A qui la leur auroit deu rendre grace.
La gent maudite aussi-tost poursuivit
Tous les pigeons, en fit ample carnage,
En dépeupla les bourgades, les champs.
Peu de prudence eurent les pauvres gens,
D'accommoder un peuple si sauvage.
Tenez toûjours divisez les méchans:
La seureté du reste de la terre
Dépend de là. Semez entre eux la guerre,
Ou vous n'aurez avec eux nulle paix.
Cecy soit dit en passant. Je me tais.

Soon did their blood rain thick and fill
The sky! (I don't exaggerate!)
Why, even if I attempted to,
My breath would fail should I relate
Every detail: the derring-do,
The daring feats, the battles fought,
The heroes felled, the carnage wrought...
They even say that, vulture-racked,
Bound to his rock, Prometheus thought
His woes were soon to end![2] In fact,
Long raged the slaughter. Pressed, attacked...
Bitten, clawed, hacked... Each side would use
Its strength, its valor, wile, and ruse
Against the other, doing its best
To swell the ranks of those consigned
To death's dank shades: the dispossessed
Of life and breath... Now, while their kind
Pursue their self-annihilation,
Birds of another feathered nation,
Mottled of breast and warm of heart—
Pigeons, I mean—will do their part
To reconcile the altercation.
Envoys are sent; their mediatory
Mission succeeds: the vultures cease
Their fray, resolve to live at peace...
Ah, but that's not quite all the story!
Soon did they turn their rage against
The ones they should have recompensed!
Pigeons, poor fools!—scores, hundreds—pay
The price, in deadly disarray,
For meddling in our cutthroats' strife!
So? Would you live a peaceful life?
Then keep your enemies at war!
A passing thought... I'll say no more.

(VII, 7)[3]

LE COCHE ET LA MOUCHE

Dans un chemin montant, sablonneux, mal-aisé,
Et de tous les côtez au Soleil exposé,
     Six forts chevaux tiroient un Coche.
Femmes, Moine, vieillards, tout estoit descendu.
L'attelage suoit, soufloit, estoit rendu.
Une Mouche survient, et des chevaux s'approche,
Prétend les animer par son bourdonnement,
Pique l'un, pique l'autre, et pense à tout moment
     Qu'elle fait aller la machine,
S'assied sur le timon, sur le nez du Cocher;
     Aussi-tost que le char chemine,
     Et qu'elle voit les gens marcher,
Elle s'en attribuë uniquement la gloire,
Va, vient, fait l'empressée; il semble que ce soit
Un Sergent de bataille allant en chaque endroit
Faire avancer ses gens, et hâter la victoire.
     La Mouche en ce commun besoin
Se plaint qu'elle agit seule, et qu'elle a tout le soin,
Qu'aucun n'aide aux chevaux à se tirer d'affaire.
     Le Moine disoit son Breviaire:
Il prenoit bien son temps! Une femme chantoit;
C'estoit bien de chansons qu'alors il s'agissoit!
Dame Mouche s'en va chanter à leurs oreilles,
     Et fait cent sotises pareilles.
Aprés bien du travail le Coche arrive au haut.
Respirons maintenant, dit la Mouche aussi-tost:
J'ay tant fait que nos gens sont enfin dans la plaine.
Çà, Messieurs les Chevaux, payez-moy de ma peine.

Ainsi certaines gens faisant les empressez
     S'introduisent dans les affaires.
     Ils font par tout les necessaires,
Et par tout importuns devroient estre chassez.

THE COACH AND THE FLY

A coach-and-six was climbing up a hill.
Rough was the road and steep. The sweltering sun
Kept beating down upon the coach until,
    At length, it stopped; and everyone—
Women, a monk, some agèd men—stepped out
To rest. The horses too, though strong and stout,
    Sweating and panting, stood exhausted...
Just then a fly flew by; stopped, stared; accosted
Each of the beasts in turn. With sting and buzz
    She goads them, thinks that what she does—
    Sitting there on the steering-shaft
    Or perching on the coachman's nose—
Will move those wheels!... The team starts up... Ah, how she throws
Herself into the fray; goes flying fore and aft,
    Here, there, up, down; plying the sergeant's craft
    At battle-stations all along the line,
        Spurring her troops to victory;
    And all the while complaining that it's she
Alone who prods them on!... Our good divine,
In fact, sits reading from his breviary
(Fine time for that!). A woman sings a tune
(Or that!)... Dame Fly, our genius military,
Hums in their ears, flits, plays her tricks... Well, soon
The coach, with toil and moil, has reached the top.
    "Ah," she sighs, "finally I can stop.
It's thanks to me they've reached their destination!"
And to the horses: "Now, *messieurs,* feel free to drop
    My well-deserved remuneration."[1]

Some pompous folk—this fable is about them!—
    Think they're essential everywhere:
To every action, cause, campaign, affair...
Best cast them out; we can well do without them.

                    (VII, 8)[2]

LES DEUX COQS

Deux Coqs vivoient en paix; une Poule survint,
    Et voila la guerre allumée.
Amour, tu perdis Troye; et c'est de toy que vint
    Cette querelle envenimée,
Où du sang des Dieux mesme on vid le Xante teint.
Long-temps entre nos Coqs le combat se maintint.
Le bruit s'en répandit par tout le voisinage.
La gent qui porte creste au spectacle accourut.
    Plus d'une Heleine au beau plumage
Fut le prix du vainqueur; le vaincu disparut.

THE TWO COCKS

Two cocks had lived in peace; but then
There came upon the scene a hen,
    And there they were, at once, at war!
O love! For you, Troy fell; though not before
The blood of gods had tinged the Xanthos red![1]
Long, too, this pair did battle. Word would spread
Through all of cockdom, and from far and near
    Their crested kinsmen would appear,
    To watch the pandemonium...
Ah, many a fair-plumed Helen will become

Il alla se cacher au fond de sa retraite,
  Pleura sa gloire et ses amours,
Ses amours, qu'un rival tout fier de sa défaite
Possedoit à ses yeux. Il voyoit tous les jours
Cet objet rallumer sa haine et son courage.
Il aiguisoit son bec, batoit l'air et ses flancs,
  Et s'exerçant contre les vents
  S'armoit d'une jalouse rage.
Il n'en eut pas besoin. Son vainqueur sur les toits
 S'alla percher, et chanter sa victoire.
  Un Vautour entendit sa voix:
  Adieu les amours et la gloire.
Tout cet orgueil perit sous l'ongle du Vautour.
  Enfin, par un fatal retour,
  Son rival autour de la Poule
  S'en revint faire le coquet:
  Je laisse à penser quel caquet,
  Car il eut des femmes en foule.
La Fortune se plaist à faire de ces coups;
Tout vainqueur insolent à sa perte travaille.
Défions-nous du sort, et prenons garde à nous
  Apres le gain d'une bataille.

The prize of our triumphant chanticleer;
While in defeat the loser—glowering, glum—
    Presents a very different story:
Skulking in ignominious retreat
To hide his shame, he mourns past loves, past glory;
Loves that his rival, gloating on his sweet
Success, enjoys before his jealous eye!
Each day he beats his flanks, sharpens his bill,
Flails with his flapping wings against the sky,
Feeding his rage, preparing for the kill…
He might as well have spared himself the trouble.
    Perched proud, above the battle's rubble,
Puffed up, the victor cocks his "doodle-doo…"
    A vulture hears his braggart cry,
Comes, swoops with taloned claw… Now, pride, good-bye!
    Glory, farewell, and loves, adieu!
    Well, don't you know? The other bird,
As fate would have it, has the final word.
Back flirting with the coop's fair belle, the latter
    Takes up where he left off, again.
(No need to tell you how much chitter-chatter
    Babble the ladies, hen to hen!)
Such are the ways of Fate: our boastful prattle
Often destroys us though we've won the battle.

                    (VII, 12)[2]

LE LION, LE LOUP, ET LE RENARD

Un Lion décrepit, gouteux, n'en pouvant plus,
Vouloit que l'on trouvât remede à la vieillesse.
Alleguer l'impossible aux Rois, c'est un abus.
    Celuy-cy parmy chaque espece
Manda des Medecins; il en est de tous arts.
Medecins au Lion viennent de toutes parts;
De tous costez luy vient des donneurs de receptes.
    Dans les visites qui sont faites,
Le Renard se dispense, et se tient clos et coy.
Le Loup en fait sa cour, daube au coucher du Roy
Son camarade absent; le Prince tout à l'heure
Veut qu'on aille enfumer Renard dans sa demeure,
Qu'on le fasse venir. Il vient, est presenté,
Et, sçachant que le Loup luy faisoit cette affaire:
Je crains, Sire, dit-il, qu'un rapport peu sincere
    Ne m'ait à mépris imputé
    D'avoir differé cet hommage;
    Mais j'estois en pelerinage,
Et m'acquitois d'un vœu fait pour vostre santé.
    Mesme j'ay veu dans mon voyage
Gens experts et sçavans, leur ay dit la langueur
Dont vostre Majesté craint à bon droit la suite:
    Vous ne manquez que de chaleur;
    Le long âge en vous l'a détruite.
D'un Loup écorché vif appliquez-vous la peau
    Toute chaude et toute fumante;

THE LION, THE WOLF, AND THE FOX

Decrepit, bent with years, and racked with gout,
The lion, most intent to find a cure
   Against old age, sent word throughout
The country's length and breadth. Now, to be sure,
   Unwise it is to tell our kings
   That there are simply certain things
That no one—none—can do! And so, in time,
Doctors of every stripe, from every clime,
Came to his side to ply their quack ideas,
   Their nostrums, and their panaceas.
   Only the fox, in fact, remained
   At home, abstaining, and refrained
From coming to put forward his opinions.
Thereat the wolf, one of the lion's minions—
One of those few admitted by his bed—[1]
   Seeing his colleague absent, said
Much ill of him; whereat the monarch sought
   To smoke him out and have him brought
Thither at once... Renard, arriving there,
Sure that the wolf had wrought the whole affair,
   Addressed the king: "Your Highness may
   Have thought—or been informed!—that I
   Care nought for his well-being. Nay, nay!
Sire, *au contraire!* Good reason is there why
I come so late. Embarked was I upon
A pilgrimage to holy shrines, thereon
To pray for your good health! While gone, indeed,

Le secret sans doute en est beau
Pour la nature défaillante.
Messire Loup vous servira,
S'il vous plaist, de robe de chambre.
Le Roy goûte cet avis-là:
On écorche, on taille, on démembre
Messire Loup. Le Monarque en soupa,
Et de sa peau s'envelopa.

Messieurs les courtisans, cessez de vous détruire:
Faites, si vous pouvez, vostre cour sans vous nuire.
Le mal se rend chez-vous au quadruple du bien.
Les daubeurs ont leur tour, d'une ou d'autre maniere:
Vous estes dans une carriere
Où l'on ne se pardonne rien.

I met many a sage. They all agreed
That warmth is what you lack, with age long fled.
A wolf's skin, steaming hot, is what you need:
'Best from the beast flayed while alive,' they said...
Sire Wolf would make a splendid dressing-gown."
   "Bully idea!" approved the Crown...
Thus was the former slain, skinned, hacked to bits.
   The latter supped on what had been
Said wolf, and wearing what had been his skin.

   Courtiers—toadies, hypocrites:
Your prattling, tattling tongues cause woes untold.
Nor it there anyone who benefits:
The ills you do return to you fourfold.
   Yours is a most precarious living:
   Unsure, unsafe, and unforgiving.

(VIII, 3)

LES OBSEQUES DE LA LIONNE

La femme du Lion mourut:
Aussi-tost chacun accourut
Pour s'aquiter envers le Prince
De certains complimens de consolation,
Qui sont surcroît d'affliction.
Il fit avertir sa Province
Que les obseques se feroient
Un tel jour, en tel lieu: ses Prevosts y seroient
Pour regler la ceremonie
Et pour placer la compagnie.
Jugez si chacun s'y trouva.
Le Prince aux cris s'abandonna,
Et tout son antre en résonna.
Les Lions n'ont point d'autre temple.
On entendit à son exemple
Rugir en leurs patois Messieurs les Courtisans.
Je definis la cour un païs où les gens,
Tristes, gais, prests à tout, à tout indifferens,
Sont ce qu'il plaist au Prince, ou, s'ils ne peuvent l'estre,
Taschent au moins de le parêtre,
Peuple caméléon, peuple singe du maître:
On diroit qu'un esprit anime mille corps;
C'est bien là que les gens sont de simples ressorts.
Pour revenir à nostre affaire,
Le Cerf ne pleura point; comment eust-il pû faire?
Cette mort le vengeoit; la Reine avoit jadis
Etranglé sa femme et son fils.
Bref il ne pleura point. Un flateur l'alla dire,
Et soûtint qu'il l'avoit veu rire.
La colere du Roy, comme dit Salomon,
Est terrible, et surtout celle du Roy Lion;
Mais ce Cerf n'avoit pas accoustumé de lire.
Le Monarque luy dit: Chetif hoste des bois,
Tu ris, tu ne suis pas ces gemissantes voix.
Nous n'appliquerons point sur tes membres profanes
Nos sacrez ongles; venez, Loups,
Vengez la Reine, immolez tous
Ce traistre à ses augustes manes.
Le Cerf reprit alors: Sire, le temps de pleurs
Est passé; la douleur est icy superfluë.
Vostre digne moitié couchée entre des fleurs,
Tout prés d'icy m'est apparuë,

THE LIONESS'S FUNERAL

Queen Lioness, King Lion's consort, died.
   Subjects came flocking to his side
   To offer their commiseration,
   Proffering words of consolation
That only made him grieve the more.
His Majesty announced throughout the nation
The regal obsequies arranged therefor;
   Proclaimed the place, the hour, the day.
   The royal provost-marshal corps
Would tend to protocol... Now (need I say?),
Courtiers, one and all, appeared in force.
The lion's den (no other church, of course,
Do lions have!) resounded with his frantic,
   Frenzied lament. His toadies, too,
Doing just what good toadies always do,
Vented their woe in echoes sycophantic,
   Each in his own patois, expressed
With much éclat and beating of the breast.
In short, a perfect image of the court:
A land whose people—be they sad or gay,
   Indifferent, unconcerned, blasé—
Become whatever suits their prince; comport
   Themselves as he requires; contort
And grimace, monkey-like, at his command;
Or, like some lizards, at his every whim,
Alter their colors to conform to him.[1]
The court, a veritable wonderland:
A thousand bodies with a single mind;
Men? No: mere springs the king has but to wind!
But I digress... Now then, of all those present,
Only the deer was disinclined to shed
The slightest tear: his wife and son were dead,
Slain by the queen in manner most unpleasant!
Her death avenged them... Tattlers even said
He laughed!... Well, quoting Solomon the Sage,
"No greater danger than a monarch's rage,
And, verily, the lion's most of all!"[2]
(The deer, however—not a reader, he—
Knew little Holy Writ, as I recall...)
"Vile beast!" the Lion thundered, angrily.
   "How dare you laugh at our distress!
   But we'll not smutch our holy claws
On such as your foul limbs!... Come, wolves! Redress

Et je l'ay d'abord reconnuë.
Amy, m'a-t-elle dit, garde que ce convoy,
Quand je vais chez les Dieux, ne t'oblige à des larmes.
Aux champs Elisiens j'ay goûté mille charmes,
Conversant avec ceux qui sont saints comme moy.
Laisse agir quelque-temps le desespoir du Roy.
J'y prens plaisir. A peine on eut oüi la chose
Qu'on se mit à crier: Miracle, apotheose.
Le Cerf eut un present, bien loin d'estre puny.
        Amusez les Rois par des songes,
Flatez-les, payez-les d'agreables mensonges.
Quelque indignation dont leur cœur soit remply,
Ils goberont l'appast, vous serez leur amy.

The insult done your queen! Take up the cause,
And immolate this wretch!" With which the deer
Quite disagreed: "Sire, weep not one more tear.
No need... A vision did I have, this hour;
I saw your gentle spouse in flowering bower,
Lying in joy. 'Good friend,' said she, 'I pray
You not permit them, on my funeral day,
To make you weep and wail!' And, in my vision,
She spoke with bliss about the fields Elysian,
With saints, like her, to keep her company.
'Let the king mourn,' she said. 'That pleases me...'"
Scarcely had he concluded than a roar
Of "Miracle!" arose. Now gifts galore,
    Instead of punishment, befell him!
Best tell the king what he would have you tell him:
Myths, fancies, lies... He'll take the bait; however
Hated you were before, now you're his friend forever.

(VIII, 14)

LE TORRENT ET LA RIVIERE

Avec grand bruit et grand fracas
Un Torrent tomboit des montagnes:
Tout fuyoit devant luy; l'horreur suivoit ses pas;
Il faisoit trembler les campagnes.
Nul voyageur n'osoit passer
Une barriere si puissante.
Un seul vid des voleurs, et se sentant presser
Il mit entre eux et luy cette onde menaçante.
Ce n'estoit que menace, et bruit, sans profondeur;
Nostre homme enfin n'eut que la peur.
Ce succés luy donnant courage,
Et les mesmes voleurs le poursuivant toûjours,
Il rencontra sur son passage
Une Riviere dont le cours,
Image d'un sommeil doux, paisible et tranquille,
Luy fit croire d'abord ce trajet fort facile.
Point de bords escarpez, un sable pur et net.
Il entre, et son cheval le met
A couvert des voleurs, mais non de l'onde noire:
Tous deux au Styx allerent boire;
Tous deux, à nâger malheureux,
Allerent traverser, au sejour tenebreux,
Bien d'autres fleuves que les nôtres.
Les gens sans bruit sont dangereux:
Il n'en est pas ainsi des autres.

THE TORRENT AND THE RIVULET

The country trembled far and wide
As lo! a mighty torrent rumbled, roared,
Tumbling its waters down the mountainside
In fearsome cataracts. Ah, woe betide
The heedless vagabond who tried to ford
Those fell, forbidding depths!... Well, one indeed
Was forced to do just that; for, seeing a pack
Of highwaymen approaching at his back,
    A certain traveler felt the need
To put said flood betwixt himself and them.
    Thanks to his daring stratagem,
    He found that he was none the worse
For fright; despite the river's clash and clatter,
    Its depth was quite another matter:
Shallow, in fact, and easy to traverse.
    Now, heartened by success (though yet
Pursued), he came upon a rivulet;
    So tranquil that it seemed asleep,
    Easy to cross: no jagged, steep,
And craggy banks... In trots our cavalier,
Astride his horse, only to disappear
Beneath its billows—calm, but oh so deep!
Saved from the brigands now, the pair must swim
Across the Stygean waters, dark and grim.
    Gushing, our torrent; hushed, our stream...
Best not judge rivers by the way they seem!
    Nor men!... Beware the still, the quiet:
Dangerous, they, much though their look belie it.

(VIII, 23)

LE SINGE ET LE LEOPARD

Le Singe avec le Léopard
    Gagnoient de l'argent à la foire:
    Ils affichoient chacun à part.
L'un d'eux disoit: Messieurs, mon merite et ma gloire
Sont connus en bon lieu; le Roy m'a voulu voir;
    Et si je meurs, il veut avoir
Un manchon de ma peau; tant elle est bigarrée,
    Pleine de taches, marquetée,
    Et vergetée, et mouchetée.
La bigarrure plaist; partant chacun le vid.
Mais ce fut bien-tost fait, bien-tost chacun sortit.
Le Singe de sa part disoit: Venez de grace,

THE APE AND THE LEOPARD

The leopard and the ape worked at the fair,
   Each one, before his stall, displaying
   Virtues unique; the former saying:
   "*Messieurs,* my fame spreads everywhere,
Unto the grandest of the *grands seigneurs.*
The king himself has come to see me! Why,
So much impressed is he, that, should I die,
   He wants to use my speckled fur—
Spotted and freckle-flecked—to make a muff."
   His audience listens, looks, admires
His coat of many colors, but soon tires
Of his harangue. When they have had enough,
   They leave to see the ape. The latter
Charms and delights them with his puff and patter:

Venez, messieurs. Je fais cent tours de passe-passe.
Cette diversité dont on vous parle tant,
Mon voisin Léopard l'a sur soy seulement;
Moy, je l'ay dans l'esprit: vostre serviteur Gille,
  Cousin et gendre de Bertrand,
  Singe du Pape en son vivant,
  Tout fraîchement en cette ville
Arrive en trois basteaux exprés pour vous parler;
Car il parle, on l'entend; il sçait danser, baler,
  Faire des tours de toute sorte,
Passer en des cerceaux; et le tout pour six blancs!
Non, Messieurs, pour un sou; si vous n'êtes contens,
Nous rendrons à chacun son argent à la porte.
Le Singe avoit raison: ce n'est pas sur l'habit
Que la diversité me plaît, c'est dans l'esprit:
L'une fournit toujours des choses agréables;
L'autre en moins d'un moment lasse les regardants.
Oh! que de grands seigneurs, au Léopard semblables,
  N'ont que l'habit pour tous talents!

"Come, step this way, *messieurs,*" says he.
    "I'll show you tricks and sleights galore,
    Hundreds you've never bargained for!…
My neighbor boasts his fine diversity.
    Indeed! The only problem is,
    All that diversity of his
Is on his back! Mine, friends is in my head!
Your faithful servant Gille am I, related
To Dom Bertrand, ape to the pope[1]—now dead
    (Alas!), but no less venerated.
    Here have I come—with three ships, mind you!—
To dance, to sing; to jump through hoops; to do
    Antics and capers of a kind you
Never would dream! And all that for one sou!
Your money back if you're not pleased!…" So went
Ape's chatter… And correctly so. For me,
    His was the true diversity:
Splendor of mind, not vain accoutrement!
Whereas, like leopard, many's the noble sire
Whose only talent lies in his attire.

                           (IX, 3)

LE TRESOR ET LES DEUX HOMMES

Un homme n'ayant plus ny credit, ny resource,
Et logeant le Diable en sa bourse,
C'est à dire, n'y logeant rien,
S'imagina qu'il feroit bien
De se pendre, et finir luy-mesme sa misere,
Puis qu'aussi bien sans luy la faim le viendroit faire,
Genre de mort qui ne duit pas
A gens peu curieux de gouster le trépas.
Dans cette intention, une vieille mazure
Fut la scene où devoit se passer l'aventure.

THE TREASURE AND THE TWO MEN

A man in dire distress pecuniary—
"The Devil," as they say, "lodged in his purse"—[1]
    Had watched his fortunes monetary
    Dwindle, in time, from bad to worse;
Until, in such a state of destitution,
    He thought, indeed, the best solution
Would be to hang himself. Said he: "So what?
Hunger will kill me if the noose does not."
    But, frankly, he was ill inclined
To such demise: it was not quite the kind
    He had envisioned as his lot.
So hanging it would be… Well, to that end

Il y porte une corde, et veut avec un clou
Au haut d'un certain mur attacher le licou.
   La muraille, vieille et peu forte,
S'ébranle aux premiers coups, tombe avec un tresor.
Nostre désesperé le ramasse, et l'emporte,
Laisse-là le licou, s'en retourne avec l'or,
Sans compter: ronde ou non, la somme plût au sire.
Tandis que le galant à grands pas se retire,
L'homme au tresor arrive et trouve son argent
     Absent.
Quoy, dit-il, sans mourir je perdray cette somme?
Je ne me pendray pas? Et vrayment si feray,
   Ou de corde je manqueray.
Le lacs estoit tout prest, il n'y manquoit qu'un homme.
Celuy-cy se l'attache, et se pend bien et beau.
   Ce qui le consola peut-estre
Fut qu'un autre eût pour luy fait les frais du cordeau.
Aussi-bien que l'argent le licou trouva maître.

L'avare rarement finit ses jours sans pleurs:
Il a le moins de part au tresor qu'il enserre,
   Thesaurizant pour les voleurs,
   Pour ses parents, ou pour la terre.
Mais que dire du troc que la fortune fit?
Ce sont-là de ses traits; elle s'en divertit.
Plus le tour est bizarre, et plus elle est contente.
   Cette Deesse inconstante
   Se mit alors en l'esprit
   De voir un homme se pendre;
   Et celuy qui se pendit
   S'y devoit le moins attendre.

He finds himself a hovel; brings a cord;
Looks for a well-placed nail; goes to suspend
The noose... Ah, but what's this? The wainscoat board
    Gives way! It falls apart... It crumbles...
Suddenly, from within the wall, out tumbles
    Treasure untold! A golden hoard!
    He scoops it up. How much? Who knows?
Enough to end his woe! And off he goes...
The one whose gold it was returned anon;
Gazed at the wall in shambles; looked around
    In anxious wonderment and found
    That all his riches, thereupon,
        Were gone![2]
    Whereon the miserly recluse,
In deep despair, and seeing there the noose—
Waiting for any neck to settle on—
Hanged himself on the spot, consoled a bit
That he'd not been obliged to pay for it.
The gold, the noose: both found someone to use them.

Avarice, greed: no miser, but that rues them
After a while! For him, what benefit
Of all his hoarded wealth? No joy, no pleasure...
Heirs, thieves, the earth itself, consume his treasure.
And what of Fate's wry twist? That goddess makes
What seem to be the oddest of mistakes—
    Intentional, of course!—to please
    Her taste for eccentricities!
    This time she had a mind to see
    A man hang by the neck; and she
    Saw one indeed. Which of the two?
    No matter. Either one would do.

(IX, 16)

L'HOMME ET LA COULEUVRE

Un homme vid une Couleuvre.
Ah! méchante, dit-il, je m'en vais faire une œuvre
Agreable à tout l'univers.
A ces mots, l'animal pervers
(C'est le serpent que je veux dire,
Et non l'homme: on pourroit aisément s'y tromper.)
A ces mots le serpent se laissant attraper
Est pris, mis en un sac, et ce qui fut le pire,
On resolut sa mort, fust-il coupable ou non.
Afin de le payer toutefois de raison,
L'autre luy fist cette harangue:
Symbole des ingrats, estre bon aux méchans,
C'est estre sot, meurs donc: ta colere et tes dents
Ne me nuiront jamais. Le Serpent en sa langue
Reprit du mieux qu'il put: S'il faloit condamner
Tous les ingrats qui sont au monde,
A qui pourroit-on pardonner?
Toy-mesme tu te fais ton procés. Je me fonde
Sur tes propres leçons; jette les yeux sur toy.
Mes jours sont en tes mains, tranche-les: ta justice
C'est ton utilité, ton plaisir, ton caprice;
Selon ces loix condamne-moy;
Mais trouve-bon qu'avec franchise
En mourant au moins je te dise
Que le symbole des ingrats
Ce n'est point le serpent, c'est l'homme. Ces paroles
Firent arrester l'autre; il recula d'un pas.
Enfin il repartit: Tes raisons sont frivoles:
Je pourrois décider; car ce droit m'appartient.
Mais rapportons nous en. —Soit fait, dit le reptile.
Une vache estoit là, l'on l'appelle, elle vient;
Le cas est proposé; c'estoit chose facile.
Faloit-il pour cela, dit-elle, m'appeller?
La Couleuvre a raison; pourquoy dissimuler?
Je nourris celuy-cy depuis longues années,
Il n'a sans mes bienfaits passé nulles journées;
Tout n'est que pour luy seul; mon lait et mes enfans
Le font à la maison revenir les mains pleines;
Mesme j'ay rétably sa santé, que les ans
Avoient alterée, et mes peines
Ont pour but son plaisir ainsi que son besoin.
Enfin me voila vieille; il me laisse en un coin

THE MAN AND THE SNAKE

A human being once saw a snake.
"Aha! Vile reprobate!" cried he.
"Here shall I now perform a courtesy
    For all the human race's sake!"
At which the vicious beast—make no mistake:
    The snake, I mean, and not the man
(Although I know how easily one can
Misjudge those words!)... Our vicious beast, in fact,
    Carelessly lets himself get caught.
    What's worse, the man, with scarce a thought
About his act, would kill said snake—now sacked
And helpless—whether guilty, whether not.
Still, he feels moved to give an explanation.
"Symbol of ingrates! Folly would it be
To treat with favor and consideration
    Those who behave depravedly.
Die, wretch! Your anger and your fangs shall never
    Harm me in any way whatever!"
To which the serpent, in his tongue, replied
    As best he could: "Sire, if we tried
To punish every ingrate, our endeavor
Never would end! Whom would we spare? It's you
    Yourself, *monsieur,* whom you condemn.
I learned your lessons and I live by them!
    Why, even now, see what you do.
My fate depends on what you think is best
For you: your pleasure, whim, self-interest...
Well, kill me if you must. But first, at least,
    Listen to what this wretched beast
Would tell you, sire, in all sincerity:
    'Symbol of ingrates,' as you say...
It's you, not I, who earn that sobriquet!"
The man stops in his tracks. "Fiddle-dee-dee!
Your life or death: the choice is mine to make!
Nevertheless, I'm willing to submit
Our case. Let others be the judge of it."
"That's fine with me. So be it," says the snake...
A cow was standing by. They put the matter
Squarely before her. "Humph!" was her reply.
    "Why waste my breath on needless chatter?
Friend serpent's cause is just. For years have I
Provided Man with wealth: he sells my milk,

Sans herbe; s'il vouloit encor me laisser paistre!
Mais je suis attachée, et si j'eusse eu pour maistre
Un serpent, eust-il sceu jamais pousser si loin
L'ingratitude? Adieu. J'ay dit ce que je pense.
L'homme tout étonné d'une telle sentence
Dit au serpent: Faut-il croire ce qu'elle dit?
C'est une radoteuse, elle a perdu l'esprit.
Croyons ce Bœuf. — Croyons, dit la rempante beste,
Ainsi dit, ainsi fait. Le Bœuf vient à pas lents.
Quand il eut ruminé tout le cas en sa teste,
        Il dit que du labeur des ans
Pour nous seuls il portoit les soins les plus pesans,
Parcourant sans cesse ce long cercle de peines
Qui revenant sur soy ramenoit dans nos plaines
Ce que Cerés nous donne, et vend aux animaux;
        Que cette suite de travaux
Pour récompense avoit, de tous tant que nous sommes,
Force coups, peu de gré; puis quand il estoit vieux,

My young… But he and all his thankless ilk
Profit therefrom, not me or mine. And when
   Age saps his strength, it's I again
   Who nurse him back to health, who serve
His pleasures and his needs! Do I deserve
My fate: grown old, to spend my waning days
Here on this grassless plot, tied to a stake
   So that I cannot even graze!
I'm sure that, had my master been a snake,
He would have shown more gratitude!… *Voilà!*
   I've had my say. Adieu." Surprised,
   The man turns to the serpent: "Ha!
Babbling old crone! You must have realized
She's lost her mind! Let's ask that ox instead."
"So be it," says the snake. And so they do…
   The loping, ponderous quadruped—
Listening, chewing on it—finally said:
   "Man is an ingrate, through and through!
For years we bear his loads, we till his fields;

On croyait l'honorer chaque fois que les hommes
Achetoient de son sang l'indulgence des Dieux.
Ainsi parla le Bœuf. L'homme dit: Faisons taire
   Cet ennuyeux déclamateur.
Il cherche de grands mots, et vient icy se faire,
   Au lieu d'arbitre, accusateur.
Je le recuse aussi. L'arbre estant pris pour juge,
Ce fut bien pis encore. Il servoit de refuge
Contre le chaud, la pluye, et la fureur des vents;
Pour nous seuls il ornoit les jardins et les champs.
L'ombrage n'estoit pas le seul bien qu'il sceust faire;
Il courboit sous les fruits; cependant, pour salaire,
Un rustre l'abattoit, c'estoit là son loyer,
Quoy que pendant tout l'an liberal il nous donne
Ou des fleurs au Printemps, ou du fruit en Automne;
L'ombre l'Esté; l'Hyver, les plaisirs du foyer.
Que ne l'émondoit-on sans prendre la cognée?
De son temperament il eust encor vécu.
L'homme trouvant mauvais que l'on l'eust convaincu,
Voulut à toute force avoir cause gagnée.
Je suis bien bon, dit-il, d'écouter ces gens-là.
Du sac et du serpent aussi-tost il donna
  Contre les murs, tant qu'il tua la beste.
   On en use ainsi chez les grands.
La raison les offense: ils se mettent en teste
Que tout est né pour eux, quadrupedes, et gens,
    Et serpens.
   Si quelqu'un desserre les dents,
C'est un sot. J'en conviens. Mais que faut-il donc faire?
   Parler de loin, ou bien se taire.

And when, thanks to our labors, Ceres yields
Her bounty, his it is! (And free, what's more!
Us, she makes pay, poor beasts, as best we can!)[1]
    And our rewards? Floggings galore!
Ah yes, ingratitude your name is Man!
He even thinks the sacrificial blocks—
On which, betimes, we bleed and die, to buy
His gods' indulgent favors—glorify
And honor our last hours." So spoke the ox.
"Enough!" exclaimed the man. "No judge is he!
    With all his pompous, boring blather,
Sooner would he my prosecutor be!"
    And so, at length, he chooses, rather,
Someone less prejudiced; to wit, a tree…
Still worse his accusations! He had been
Man's refuge from the heat, the wind, the rain;
Joy of his flowering garden, fruited plain:
    No season of the year wherein
He had not served Man's needs. And for his pain?
Hacked down by bumpkins! Slain, not simply pruned
And left to live his life!… Accused, impugned,
Angered at his defeat, taken aback,
Man sneers: "How kind it was of me to take
The time to hear those churls!" then hurls the sack
    Against a wall, and kills the snake.
Such are, alack! the powerful. They make
A mockery of reason, will not hear it.
Everything, everyone exists to do
        Their will. (Snakes too!)
    You go to speak the truth? They jeer it.
"Yes," you say. "Well then, what to do withal?"
Speak at a distance… Or don't speak at all.

                    (X, 1)

L'ENFOUISSEUR ET SON COMPERE

Un Pinsemaille avoit tant amassé
Qu'il ne sçavoit où loger sa finance.
L'avarice, compagne et sœur de l'ignorance,
Le rendoit fort embarassé
Dans le choix d'un dépositaire;
Car il en vouloit un. Et voicy sa raison.
L'objet tente; il faudra que ce monceau s'altere,
Si je le laisse à la maison;
Moy-mesme de mon bien je seray le larron.
Le larron, quoy joüir, c'est se voler soy-mesme!
Mon amy, j'ai pitié de ton erreur extrême;
Apprend de moy cette leçon:
Le bien n'est bien qu'en tant que l'on s'en peut défaire.
Sans cela c'est un mal. Veux-tu le reserver
Pour un âge et des temps qui n'en ont plus que faire?
La peine d'acquerir, le soin de conserver,
Ostent le prix à l'or, qu'on croit si necessaire.
Pour se décharger d'un tel soin,
Nostre homme eust pû trouver des gens surs au besoin;
Il aima mieux la terre, et prenant son compere,
Celuy-cy l'aide. Ils vont enfoüir le tresor.
Au bout de quelque-temps l'homme va voir son or:
Il ne retrouva que le giste.
Soupçonnant à bon droit le compere, il va viste
Luy dire: Apprestez-vous; car il me reste encor
Quelques deniers; je veux les joindre à l'autre masse.
Le Compere aussi-tost va remettre en sa place
L'argent volé, prétendant bien
Tout reprendre à la fois sans qu'il y manquast rien.
Mais pour ce coup l'autre fut sage:
Il retint tout chez luy, résolu de joüir,
Plus n'entasser, plus n'enfoüir.
Et le pauvre voleur, ne trouvant plus son gage,
Pensa tomber de sa hauteur.
Il n'est pas mal-aisé de tromper un trompeur.

THE MONEY-BURIER AND HIS FRIEND[1]

A most close-fisted miser had amassed
    Great wealth; but he was puzzled, very,
As to his choice of a depositary,
One who would keep it safe and hold it fast.
(Dull-wittedness and avarice are kin!)
    Thought he: "Find such a one I must.
My house is not a proper place wherein
To store my pelf. I cannot even trust
Myself not to purloin—oh, heaven forfend it!—
A coin from time to time; aye, even spend it!"
    "Oh?" would I ask him. Can it be
You think of spending as self-thievery?
Folly, poor friend, it is; pure foolishness!
    Best learn: wealth is not wealth unless
We put it to some useful end; if not,
    It's but a useless burden.[2] What?
Would you toil for your fortune, pile your gold,
Waiting to use it ('By and by... Anon...')
    Until that day when, rich but old,
    You've nothing left to spend it on?"
Many a trusty soul he could have found,
Who would have proven equal to the task
    Should he have merely thought to ask.
    Instead he chose to trust the ground:
With faithful friend he digs, buries it all...
Later he yearns to view his hoard; but there
Finds nothing but the hole! Suspicions fall—
    As fall they ought!—on his *compère*.
"More coins," he tells him, "must you help me hide."
    Whereat the latter—gulled, green-eyed—
Restores the stolen fortune to the spot,
Intending, later, to come steal the lot.
    Our miser, though, this time is wary;
Now he remains his own depositary,
No more to bury but to spend his treasure.
    Friend thief, returning at his leisure,
Finding the booty gone, stands foiled, defeated.
How easily the cheat, in turn, is cheated!

                      (X, 4)

LA PERDRIX ET LES COCS

Parmy de certains Cocs incivils, peu galans,
    Toûjours en noise et turbulens,
    Une Perdrix estoit nourrie.
    Son sexe et l'hospitalité,
De la part de ces Cocs peuple à l'amour porté
Luy faisoient esperer beaucoup d'honnesteté:
Ils feroient les honneurs de la mesnagerie.
Ce peuple cependant, fort souvent en furie,
Pour la Dame étrangere ayant peu de respec,
Luy donnoit fort souvent d'horribles coups de bec.
    D'abord elle en fut affligée;
Mais si-tost qu'elle eut vû cette troupe enragée
S'entrebattre elle-mesme, et se percer les flancs,
Elle se consola: Ce sont leurs mœurs, dit-elle,
Ne les accusons point; plaignons plûtost ces gens.
    Jupiter sur un seul modele
    N'a pas formé tous les esprits:
Il est des naturels de Cocs et de Perdrix.
S'il dépendoit de moy, je passerois ma vie
    En plus honneste compagnie.
Le maistre de ces lieux en ordonne autrement.
    Il nous prend avec des tonnelles,
Nous loge avec des Cocs, et nous coupe les aisles:
C'est de l'homme qu'il faut se plaindre seulement.

THE PARTRIDGE AND THE COCKS

A partridge had been placed to feed
   With one of the most raucous flocks
Of ungallant, uncouth, and rowdy cocks,
    Ill-bred exemplars of their breed.
Now, laws of hospitality decreed
(Or so she thought!) that, being a lady, she
    Ought to be treated civilly
By those well known for amorous inclination…
Not so! Not only did they not respect her;
Often, so great their state of excitation,
That with their piercing bills they poked and pecked her!
    Troubled at first, in time she saw
Our cocks have at each other, beak and claw,
Fighting amongst themselves. "Ah," she opined,
"Such are, I fear, the customs of their kind."
    Somewhat consoled, she adds: "In sum,
More to be pitied than condemned are they!
Behold! Jove did not form all poultrydom
    From one design: cocks, some become;
Partridges, others… If I had my way,
    I'd live in worthier company!
Alas, our master does not quite agree.
He nets us; clips our wings; then, come what may,
    He coops us with these fowl, *ad hoc:*
It's man we should complain of, not the cock!"

(X, 7)

LE VIEILLARD
ET LES TROIS JEUNES HOMMES

Un octogenaire plantoit.
Passe encor de bastir; mais planter à cét âge!
Disoient trois jouvenceaux enfans du voisinage;
Assurement il radotoit.
Car, au nom des Dieux, je vous prie,
Quel fruict de ce labeur pouvez-vous recüeillir?
Autant qu'un Patriarche il vous faudroit vieillir.
A quoy bon charger vostre vie
Des soins d'un avenir qui n'est pas fait pour vous?
Ne songez desormais qu'à vos erreurs passées:
Quittez le long espoir, et les vastes pensées;
Tout cela ne convient qu'à nous.
Il ne convient pas à vous mesmes,
Repartit le Vieillard. Tout établissement
Vient tard et dure peu. La main des Parques blesmes
De vos jours et des miens se joüé également.
Nos termes sont pareils par leur courte durée.

THE OLD MAN
AND THE THREE YOUNG MEN

An old man (eighty years or more)
Was in his orchard, planting. Three young men—
Three village swains—were heard to say: "What for,
For heaven's sake?… Him? Plant?… Now then,
Build, maybe… But to plant? At his age? Why?
He must be daft!" Then, to the elder: "Friend,
For all your toil, what fruits do you pretend
To come and gather by and by?
Enjoy the patriarch's repose. Why fuss
And fret for times you'll never know?
Dream of those wild oats sown long years ago,
Not of the future: that belongs to us."
"To you?" the old man answered. "Oh?
Not so… The ashen-fingered Fates make sport
Of everyone—me, you—quite equally.
The time allotted all of us is short.
Can one of us be sure that he
Will be the last to view the firmament

Qui de nous des clartez de la voûte azurée
Doit joüir le dernier? Est-il aucun moment
Qui vous puisse assurer d'un second seulement?
Mes arriere-neveux me devront cét ombrage:
          Hé bien défendez-vous au Sage
De se donner des soins pour le plaisir d'autruy?
Cela mesme est un fruict que je gouste aujourd'huy:
J'en puis joüir demain, et quelques jours encore;
          Je puis enfin compter l'Aurore
          Plus d'une fois sur vos tombeaux.
Le Vieillard eut raison; l'un des trois jouvenceaux
Se noya dés le port allant à l'Amerique;
L'autre afin de monter aux grandes dignitez,
Dans les emplois de Mars servant la Republique,
Par un coup impréveu vid ses jours emportez.
          Le troisiéme tomba d'un arbre
          Que luy-mesme il voulut enter;
Et pleurez du Vieillard, il grava sur leur marbre
          Ce que je viens de raconter.

In azured splendor?... No, each moment spent
Might be our last; and yours no less than mine.
What's more, one day this tree I plant, this vine,
Will cool my progeny. Its shade will be
   My gift to them. Would you deprive
The wise man of the joy, whilst yet alive,
To see the boon he grants posterity?
I take that pleasure now; tomorrow too,
Perhaps; and even longer. As for you,
Who knows how many a dawn I'll live to see
Rising above your graves?..." His words came true:
   Gone, soon, all three, as he had reckoned!
Off to America, the first one, drowned;
In Mars' employ, felled on the battleground,
Seeking his country's accolade, the second;
The third, climbing a tree to graft a limb,
Fallen and killed... The old man, so they tell,
   Shed many a mournful tear for him,
   And for the other two as well.
He lived to see their tombstones consecrated,
And graven with the story I've related.[1]

(XI, 8)

LE RENARD, LES MOUCHES, ET
LE HERISSON

Aux traces de son sang, un vieux hôte des bois,
      Renard fin, subtil, et matois,
Blessé par des Chasseurs et tombé dans la fange,
Autrefois attira ce Parasite aîlé
      Que nous avons Mouche appellé.
Il accusoit les Dieux, et trouvoit fort étrange
Que le sort à tel poinct le voulût affliger
      Et le fist aux Mouches manger.
Quoy! se jetter sur moi, sur moi le plus habile
      De tous les Hôtes des Forêts?
Depuis quand les Renards sont-ils un si bon mets?
Et que me sert ma queuë? est-ce un poids inutile?
Va! le Ciel te confonde, animal importun.
      Que ne vis-tu sur le commun!
      Un Herisson du voisinage,
      Dans mes Vers nouveau personnage,
Voulut le délivrer de l'importunité
      Du peuple plein d'avidité.
Je les vais de mes dards enfiler par centaines,
Voisin Renard, dit-il, et terminer tes peines.
—Garde-t'en bien, dit l'autre; ami, ne le fais pas;
Laisse-les, je te prie, achever leur repas.
Ces animaux sont saouls: une troupe nouvelle
Viendroit fondre sur moi, plus âpre et plus cruelle.
Nous ne trouvons que trop de mangeurs ici-bas:
Ceux-cy sont courtisans, ceux-là sont magistrats.
Aristote appliquoit cet apologue aux hommes.
      Les exemples en sont communs,
      Sur tout au pays où nous sommes.
Plus telles gens sont pleins, moins ils sont importuns.

THE FOX, THE FLIES, AND
THE HEDGEHOG

Wounded by hunters, left to die,
Renard (one of the woodland's wily best!),
Mired in the muck, falls victim to that pest,
That wingèd parasite we call the fly—
Attracted by his bloody trail, come by
    To dine! The old fox, sore distressed
At her attack, rails at the gods, decries
A fate so hostile that, alas, it lets
    The likes of him be food for flies!
    "Me? Me?" he wails. "Alack," he frets.
    "Me, craftiest creature in the wood?
Is fox considered such a savory meal?
And my poor tail! Ah, if I only could
    Flail it about as flail I should,
    Then, irksome insects, would you feel
My awesome wrath! Be damned, vile enemy!
Go feed on common folk and let me be!…"
A hedgehog from the neighborhood—a new
Character in my verse![1]—thought he might do
    The fox a kindly courtesy
And rid him of the beasts importunate.
"Neighbor," said he, "I'll shoot a quill, and spear
    Hundreds at once!" "No, please, compeer!"
Said fox. "That would be most unfortunate.
Leave these to glut their fill. They're almost sated.
But should they go, others will surely come—
Worse still, the cruelest in all insectdom!—
To take the places they shall have vacated."
Numerous, too, our pests of human sort:
    Magistrates, sycophants at court—
    And all of them the hungriest!
It's Aristotle's tale I tell.[2] But it
Offers a moral for our time. To wit:
They harass least who fill their bellies best!

(XII, 13)

LA FOREST ET LE BUCHERON

Un Bucheron venoit de rompre ou d'égarer
Le bois dont il avoit emmanché sa coignée.
Cette perte ne put si-tôt se reparer
Que la Forest n'en fût quelque-tems épargnée.
    L'Homme enfin la prie humblement
    De lui laisser tout doucement
    Emporter une unique branche,
    Afin de faire un autre manche.
Il iroit emploïer ailleurs son gagne pain;
Il laisseroit debout maint Chêne et maint Sapin
Dont chacun respectoit la vieillesse et les charmes.
L'innocente Forest lui fournit d'autres armes.
Elle en eut du regret. Il emmanche son fer.
    Le miserable ne s'en sert
    Qu'à dépoüiller sa bien-faitrice
    De ses principaux ornemens.
    Elle gémit à tous momens:
    Son propre don fait son supplice.

Voilà le train du Monde et de ses Sectateurs;
On s'y sert du bienfait contre les bienfaiteurs.
Je suis las d'en parler; mais que de doux ombrages
    Soient exposez à ces outrages,
    Qui ne se plaindroit là-dessus?
Helas! j'ai beau crier et me rendre incommode:
    L'ingratitude et les abus
    N'en seront pas moins à la mode.

THE FOREST AND THE WOODSMAN

A woodsman broke the handle of his axe—
Or lost it. (I'm not certain which: no matter…)
Until the former could replace the latter,
Safe was the forest from his hews and hacks,
    His chops and chips, his splitting blows…
    But soon the canny woodsman goes
    Back to the forest; asks her, please,
In all humility, to let him take
One single branch from any of her trees—
    Just one—so that he might remake
His tool, therewith to earn his livelihood
Far from her fine and venerable wood.
Indeed, no more to fell her would he use it!
The forest hears his pleas and, being good
And kind (rather, naïve!) cannot refuse it.
Woodsman takes bough… Repairs his axe… Ah, me!
Soon has he stripped his benefactress bare,
    And leaves her, moaning, lying there,
Brought down by her own magnanimity.

So goes the world and all too many in it—
How often must I sing the same refrain?—
Do a good turn, they turn on you next minute!
But this? To ravage nature's sweet domain,
Her groves, her shades!… Who can, unmoved, behold
    Such devastation?[1] Yes, I scold,
I rage… But what's the use? Complain… Complain…
Vice and ingratitude—for all my passion,
Rant though I may—will long remain the fashion.

                     (XII, 16)

LE RENARD, LE LOUP, ET LE CHEVAL

Un Renard jeune encor, quoique des plus madrez,
Vid le premier Cheval qu'il eût vû de sa vie.
Il dit à certain Loup, franc novice: Accourez:
    Un Animal paît dans nos prez,
Beau, grand; j'en ai la vuë encor toute ravie.
  —Est-il plus fort que nous? dit le Loup en riant.
    Fais-moi son Portrait, je te prie.
  —Si j'étois quelque Peintre ou quelque Etudiant,
Repartit le Renard, j'avancerois la joie
    Que vous aurez en le voïant.
Mais venez. Que sçait-on? Peut-être est-ce une proie
    Que la Fortune nous envoie.
Ils vont; et le Cheval, qu'à l'herbe on avoit mis,
Assez peu curieux de semblables amis,
Fut presque sur le point d'enfiler la venelle.
Seigneur, dit le Renard, vos humbles serviteurs
Apprendroient volontiers comment on vous appelle.
Le Cheval, qui n'étoit dépourvû de cervelle,
Leur dit: Lisez mon nom, vous le pouvez, Messieurs;
Mon Cordonnier l'a mis autour de ma semelle.
Le Renard s'excusa sur son peu de sçavoir.
Mes parens, reprit-il, ne m'ont point fait instruire;
Ils sont pauvres, et n'ont qu'un trou pour tout avoir.
Ceux du Loup, gros Messieurs, l'ont fait apprendre à lire.
    Le Loup, par ce discours flaté,
    S'approcha; mais sa vanité
Luy coûta quatre dents: le Cheval lui desserre

THE FOX, THE WOLF, AND THE HORSE

A fox—quite young, but still quite clever—
Happened upon a horse, the first one ever
   His youthful eyes had seen. Close by
He spied a wolf—young, too, and most naïve!
"Out there!" he cried. "Come, friend! I can't believe
My eyes! Some beast or other, grazing… Why,
I never saw one of such size before!
Beautiful too!…" "Haw!" scoffed the wolf. "Is he
Stronger than me and you? Do tell me more!
Describe him." And the fox's repartee:
"I wouldn't do him justice! If I were
A painter, or some studious connoisseur,
   I should, with pleasure, have extolled him
   Even before you could behold him!
Come and see for yourself! Who knows? He may
Be sent by Fortune; some new, tasty prey!"
So off they go… The horse, still browsing there,
   But just about to leave, a-trot,
   Thinks precious little of our pair;
Cares not, indeed, one tittle, not one jot.
"*Seigneur,*" says fox with courtly air, "we two,
Your humble servants, would be pleased to know
Your name." The horse, a canny sort, says: "Oh?
My name *messieurs*? It's written on my shoe.
My cobbler put it there. Come read it." "Who?"
Says fox. "Not me. I never learned my letters.
   Nought could my parents pay, poor debtors!
Whereas Sire Wolf's… Noble and rich are they!
He learned to read!" The wolf, proud popinjay,

Un coup; et haut le pied. Voilà mon Loup par terre,
        Mal en point, sanglant et gâté.
Frere, dit le Renard, ceci nous justifie
        Ce que m'ont dit des gens d'esprit:
Cet animal vous a sur la machoire écrit
Que de tout inconnu le Sage se méfie.

Drew near… Looked… Peered… Dear me! His vanity
Cost him four teeth, as horse let fly a hoof;
    And wolf, with many an "ayyy!" and "ouf!"
    Laid low, lay bloodied, hoodwinked he!
Meanwhile the horse turned tail and off he sprinted.
    "Friend," said the fox, eager to show him
How he had erred, "now is your jaw imprinted:
'Best not to trust the stranger till you know him!'"[1]

(XII, 17)

LE RENARD ET LES POULETS D'INDE

Contre les assauts d'un Renard
Un arbre à des Dindons servoit de citadelle.
Le perfide, aïant fait tout le tour du rempart
Et vû chacun en sentinelle,
S'écria: Quoi! ces gens se mocqueront de moi!
Eux seuls seront exemts de la commune loi!
Non, par tous les Dieux, non. Il accomplit son dire.
La Lune alors luisant sembloit contre le Sire
Vouloir favoriser la Dindonniere gent.
Lui qui n'étoit novice au métier d'assiégeant,
Eut recours à son sac de ruses scelerates,
Feignit vouloir gravir, se guinda sur ses pattes,
Puis contrefit le mort, puis le ressuscité.
Harlequin n'eût executé
Tant de differens personnages.
Il élevoit sa queuë, il la faisoit briller,
Et cent mille autres badinages,
Pendant quoi nul Dindon n'eût osé sommeiller:
L'ennemi les lassoit, en leur tenant la vûë
Sur même objet toûjours tenduë.
Les pauvres gens étant à la longue éblouïs,
Toûjours il en tomboit quelqu'un: autant de pris,
Autant de mis à part; prés de moitié succombe.
Le Compagnon les porte en son garde-manger.
Le trop d'attention qu'on a pour le danger
Fait le plus souvent qu'on y tombe.

THE FOX AND THE YOUNG TURKEY COCKS

One night, a brood of youngster turkey cocks,[1]
Fleeing the onslaughts of a certain fox,
Took refuge in a tree—*détresse oblige!*—
    Round which Renard, quick to lay siege,
Went circling, glaring up at each one, perching
Sentinel-like. "Gadzooks!" cried he. "What sort
    Of folk are these, to be besmirching
    My reputation, making sport
Of me! What makes them think their foul cohort
Can flout the rules! By all the gods, we'll see!"
Now then, it happened that the moon shone bright—
So much the better for our company
(Fowl cohort,[2] they!). And so, no neophyte,
    The fox goes searching through his sack
Of hoax and trick; first feigns to climb the tree;
    Pretends to fall, flat on his back—
    Dead, he would have the turkeys think;
Then lurching up, revived, quick as a wink,
Lifts high his shining tail to charm their gaze;
Holds their attention…[3] (Even Harlequin—
    Consummate actor—would have been
Hard put to act as well![4]) Anon, a-daze—
Staring, yet daring not to sleep—first one,
Then two, then more fall to the ground, undone.
    In time, half of the brood, at least,
Lies in a heap before our fox artiste,
Who takes them to his larder, stocks his lair…
    When danger threatens, yes, take care;
    But careful lest you overdo it:
Too much, and you may well fall victim to it.

(XII, 18)

LE PHILOSOPHE SCITHE

Un Philosophe austere, et né dans la Scithie,
Se proposant de suivre une plus douce vie,
Voïagea chez les Grecs, et vid en certains lieux
Un Sage assez semblable au vieillard de Virgile,
Homme égalant les Rois, homme approchant des Dieux,
Et, comme ces derniers satisfait et tranquile.
Son bonheur consistoit aux beautez d'un Jardin.
Le Scithe l'y trouva, qui la serpe à la main,
De ses arbres à fruit retranchoit l'inutile,
Ebranchoit, émondoit, ôtoit ceci, cela,
        Corrigeant par tout la Nature,
Excessive à païer ses soins avec usure.
        Le Scithe alors lui demanda
Pourquoi cette ruïne. Etoit-il d'homme sage
De mutiler ainsi ces pauvres habitants?

THE SCYTHIAN PHILOSOPHER

A Scythian philosopher there was—
Dour and austere—who took it in his mind
To leave his rugged native land behind
And go to live among the Greeks; because
With them he thought that he would surely find
A kinder, gentler life… Once there, our Scyth
Happened upon an old man, bent with age,
But king-like, god-like—much as Virgil's sage,[1]
Calm and serene—who, hook in hand, therewith
    Was pruning, thinning out his trees:
Here a branch, there a bough, a useless limb—
Correcting nature's lush excesses. "Please,"
He asks the elder, drawing close to him,
"Why this destruction? Is it wise of you
To tear apart these poor things so? Look!… Look
At what you've done! Come, come… Put down your hook;
Let Time's scythe do its work. Their days are few:

Quittez-moi vôtre serpe, instrument de dommage;
    Laissez agir la faux du temps:
Ils iront aussi-tôt border le noir rivage.
J'ôte le superflu, dit l'autre, et, l'abatant,
    Le reste en profite d'autant.
Le Scithe, retourné dans sa triste demeure,
Prend la serpe à son tour, coupe et taille à toute heure;
Conseille à ses voisins, prescrit à ses amis
    Un universel abatis.
Il ôte de chez luy les branches les plus belles,
Il tronque son Verger contre toute raison,
    Sans observer temps ni saison,
    Lunes ni vieilles ni nouvelles.
Tout languit et tout meurt. Ce Scithe exprime bien
    Un indiscret Stoïcien.
    Celui-ci retranche de l'ame
Desirs et passions, le bon et le mauvais,
    Jusqu'aux plus innocens souhaits.
Contre de telles gens, quant à moi, je reclame.
Ils ôtent à nos cœurs le principal ressort:
Ils font cesser de vivre avant que l'on soit mort.

Soon will they cross the Styx's dark abyss
    Without your help!" "You talk amiss,"
Replies the sage. "My task is to remove
    The useless growth, and thus improve
All of the rest..." At length the Scyth returned
To Scythian climes. He thinks of what he learned,
Decides to practice it; hacks here, snips there,
Uproots, cuts, slashes, rips, and soon lays bare
    His orchard. Full the moon or new,
    Whatever month, whatever season—
Scraggy his trees or stout: no rhyme, no reason,
    Pull them all out!... His neighbors too,
At his suggestion, do the same as he;
Until what once was garden, grove, and wood
Lies ravaged, dead... This Scyth recalls to me
One of those Stoics, whose philosophy
Casts every passion from our soul: the good,
The evil; who, in their foolhardihood,
    Purge all desire; whose tongues decry
Even the innocent; who, if they could,
Would banish heart's most precious fire; who try
To make us cease to live, even before we die.

(XII, 20)

L'ELEPHANT ET LE SINGE DE JUPITER

Autrefois l'Elephant et le Rinoceros,
En dispute du pas et des droits de l'Empire,
Voulurent terminer la querelle en champ clos.
Le jour en étoit pris, quand quelqu'un vint leur dire
   Que le Singe de Jupiter,
Portant un Caducée, avoit paru dans l'air.
Ce Singe avoit nom Gille, à ce que dit l'Histoire.
   Aussi-tôt l'Elephant de croire
   Qu'en qualité d'Ambassadeur
   Il venoit trouver sa Grandeur.
   Tout fier de ce sujet de gloire,
Il attend Maître Gille, et le trouve un peu lent
   A luy presenter sa créance.
   Maître Gille enfin en passant
   Va saluër son Excellence.
L'autre étoit preparé sur la légation;
   Mais pas un mot: l'attention
Qu'il croïoit que les Dieux eussent à sa querelle
N'agitoit pas encor chez eux cette nouvelle.

THE ELEPHANT AND JUPITER'S APE

The elephant and the rhinoceros,
    Years past, were raising quite a fuss,
    Disputing matters monarchistic—
Succession, kingly powers, and such. And so
    They took it in their heads to go
Behind closed doors, in combat pugilistic,
Bare hoof to hoof... Before the fateful day
When they are to engage in their endeavor,
    Someone comes to announce, however,
That, flying through the air, Jove's ape—they say
    His name was Gille[1]—has just been seen,
Bearing the godly scepter. "Ah, *au fait,*"
Exults the elephant. "Then that must mean
    He's coming as an emissary
To see My Majesty plenipotentiary!"
    He waits... And waits... But Master Gille shows no
Intention, not the slightest inclination,
To come present his formal creditation.
At length, when he drops by to say hello,

      Qu'importe à ceux du Firmament
        Qu'on soit Mouche ou bien Elephant?
Il se vid donc reduit à commencer lui-même.
Mon cousin Jupiter, dit-il, verra dans peu
Un assez beau combat de son Trône suprême.
      Toute sa Cour verra beau jeu.
—Quel combat? dit le Singe avec un front severe.
L'Elephant repartit: Quoi! vous ne sçavez pas
Que le Rinoceros me dispute le pas;
Qu'Elephantide a guerre avecque Rinocere?
Vous connoissez ces lieux: ils ont quelque renom.
—Vraiment, je suis ravi d'en apprendre le nom,
Repartit Maître Gille; on ne s'entretient guere
De semblables sujets dans nos vastes Lambris.
      L'Elephant honteux et surpris
Lui dit: Et parmi nous que venez-vous donc faire?
—Partager un brin d'herbe entre quelques Fourmis.
Nous avons soin de tout; et quant à vôtre affaire,
On n'en dit rien encor dans le conseil des Dieux.
Les petits et les grands sont égaux à leurs yeux.

The elephant expects his mediation.
    Again he waits… And waits… But not
    One word about his battle. "What?
Who would believe the gods could care so little
About my fight? What? Not one jot or tittle?"
Indeed! What matters to the gods on high
    If one be elephant or fly!
And so it fell to him himself to start
    Their chat: "My royal counterpart—
My cousin Jupiter—and all his court
Soon will see combat of the fiercest sort!"
"Combat?" retorts the ape, a-scowl. Wherefore
The elephant replies: "No! Can it be
    That you know nothing of the war
Between fair Elephrance and foul Rhinocery?
    Surely you know our nations!" "Oh? Somehow,"
Says Gille, "I didn't, but I'm glad to now…
Up there, in our vast halls, we seldom deal
With trifles!" Elephant, chagrined: "Then why
    Did you come down?" And Master Gille:
"To bring some ants a leaf, give them their meal;[2]
Your silly spat hasn't yet caught Jove's eye.
    In time, no doubt, it will withal:
The gods tend all their subjects, great and small."[3]

(XII, 21)

LA MATRONE D'EPHESE

S'il est un conte usé, commun, et rebatu,
C'est celui qu'en ces Vers j'accommode à ma guise.
        Et pourquoi donc le choisis-tu?
        Qui t'engage à cette entreprise?
N'a-t-elle point déja produit assez d'ecrits?
        Quelle grace aura ta Matrone
        Au prix de celle de Pétrone?
Comment la rendras-tu nouvelle à nos esprits?
Sans répondre aux censeurs, car c'est chose infinie,
Voyons si dans mes Vers je l'aurai rajeunie.

        Dans Ephese il fut autrefois
Une Dame en sagesse et vertus sans égale,
        Et selon la commune voix
Aïant scû rafiner sur l'amour conjugale.
Il n'estoit bruit que d'elle et de sa chasteté:
        On l'alloit voir par rareté;
C'étoit l'honneur du sexe: heureuse sa patrie!
Chaque Mere à sa Bru l'alleguoit pour patron;
Chaque Epoux la prônoit à sa Femme cherie:
D'elle descendent ceux de la Prudoterie,
        Antique et celebre maison.
        Son mari l'aimoit d'amour folle.
        Il mourut. De dire comment,
        Ce seroit un détail frivole;
        Il mourut, et son testament
N'étoit plein que de legs qui l'auroient consolée,
Si les biens réparoient la perte d'un Mari
        Amoureux autant que cheri.
Mainte Veuve pourtant fait la déchevelée,
Qui n'abandonne pas le soin du demeurant,
Et du bien qu'elle aura fait le compte en pleurant.
Celle-ci par ses cris mettoit tout en alarme;
        Celle-cy faisoit un vacarme,
Un bruit, et des regrets à percer tous les cœurs;
        Bien qu'on sçache qu'en ces malheurs,
De quelque desespoir qu'une ame soit atteinte,
La douleur est toûjours moins forte que la plainte:
Toûjours un peu de faste entre parmi les pleurs.
Chacun fit son devoir de dire à l'affligée
Que tout a sa mesure, et que de tels regrets
        Pourroient pécher par leur excés:

THE MATRON OF EPHESUS

If any tale—well worn, banal—
Needs no retelling, it's the one I shall
   Herewith relate in my own wise.
   "But why?" you ask. "Why re-create her,
That personage of more than one narrator:
The Matron that Petronius glorifies
And many an imitator, too, discusses?[1]
What special grace can you give yours to vie,
   Verily, with Petronius's?"
Rather than face my critics in reply—
   Task of duration infinite!—
   Let me but try to see if I
Can spruce his famous Matron up a bit.

Long years gone by, in Ephesus,
There lived a woman, passing virtuous,
In wifely duty chaste beyond compare:
Pride of her sex, hailed far and wide. And thus
   Came many a soul to see her there,
Eager to gaze upon a sight so rare.
Each mother wished such consort for her son;
Each man wished for a mate like such a one.
(Ancestress of the clan Prudenda, she
   Gave rise to long posterity…[2])
   Her husband loved her madly. But
   He died—no need to say of what
   (Frivolous piece of information!);
   He died: let that suffice—and left
A will that would have brought much consolation
Could wealth console Madame, now sore bereft
Of spouse so loving and so loved. But no,
Not such a widow, she: such as will crow
   Their grief—hair torn and garments rent—
But who, beating their breast to loud lament,
Add up their riches as they weep their woe.
No, this one moaned and wailed and bellowed so,
That all grew much alarmed and much distressed.
   (Though they assumed that, like the rest,
This widow, while sincere her lamentation,
Was not ungiven to exaggeration,
Just for the show.) And thus they did as best
   They could to temper her chagrin,

Chacun rendit par là sa douleur rengregée.
Enfin ne voulant plus jouïr de la clarté
     Que son Epoux avoit perduë,
Elle entre dans sa tombe, en ferme volonté
D'accompagner cette ombre aux enfers descenduë.
Et voïez ce que peut l'excessive amitié,
(Ce mouvement aussi va jusqu'à la folie);
Une Esclave en ce lieu la suivit par pitié,
     Prête à mourir de compagnie;
Prête, je m'entends bien, c'est-à-dire, en un mot,

Telling Her Widowhood it was a sin
To mourn beyond all proper measure. Yet
    All they accomplished was to whet
The dire despair of our fair heroine,
    And make her grieve, alas, the more;
Until, in time, the poor bereaved forswore
The light of day, loath to participate
In pleasure now denied her lifeless mate.
And so into his tomb went she, intent
    There to remain and join the late
Lamented in his netherward descent.
With her there went a slave girl, much devoted—

N'aïant examiné qu'à demi ce complot,
Et jusques à l'effet courageuse et hardie.
L'Esclave avec la Dame avoit été nourrie.
Toutes deux s'entraimoient, et cette passion
Etoit cruë avec l'âge au cœur des deux femelles:
Le Monde entier à peine eut fourni deux modeles
   D'une telle inclination.

Comme l'Esclave avoit plus de sens que la Dame,
Elle laissa passer les premiers mouvemens,
Puis tâcha, mais en vain, de remettre cette ame
Dans l'ordinaire train des communs sentimens.
Aux consolations la Veuve inaccessible
S'appliquoit seulement à tout moïen possible
De suivre le Défunt aux noirs et tristes lieux.
Le fer auroit été le plus court et le mieux;
Mais la Dame vouloit paître encore ses yeux
   Du tresor qu'enfermoit le biere,
   Froide dépoüille, et pourtant chere:
   C'étoit-là le seul aliment
   Qu'elle prît en ce monument.
   La faim donc fut celle des portes
   Qu'entre d'autres de tant de sortes
Nôtre Veuve choisit pour sortir d'ici-bas.
Un jour se passe, et deux sans autre nourriture
Que ses profonds soupirs, que ses frequents helas,
   Qu'un inutile et long murmure
Contre les Dieux, le sort, et toute la nature.
   Enfin sa douleur n'obmit rien,
  Si la douleur doit s'exprimer si bien.

Encore un autre mort faisoit sa residence
Non loin de ce tombeau, mais bien differemment,
   Car il n'avoit pour monument
   Que le dessous d'une potence:
Pour exemple aux voleurs on l'avoit là laissé.
   Un soldat bien récompensé
   Le gardoit avec vigilance.
   Il étoit dit par Ordonnance
Que si d'autres voleurs, un parent, un ami,
L'enlevoient, le Soldat nonchalant, endormi,
   Rempliroit aussi-tôt sa place.

Cradle-companion, close as close could be—
Thither to keep her mistress company
    And die as well; though, be it noted,
    This loving, loyal devotee
("Devoted?" Rather "mad," if you ask me!),
Exemplar of affection sisterly,[3]
Had failed, I fear, to think the matter through.

But soon the servant comes to realize
What such a stay must needs expose her to.
At first she lets her mistress sigh her sighs
    And groan her groans; then vainly tries
To make her mourn as other widows do,
In manner more conventional withal.
The Matron, though—obdurate, spurning all
The usual consolations—has one thought
    And one alone: what means she ought
    Employ to reach unto that dismal
    Valley of death, domain abysmal.
    Quickest, no doubt, would be the sword.
But she demurs; for she would longer feast
    Her eyes upon the poor deceased—
Cold in his bier, and yet no less adored.
Such being, indeed, the only nourishment
    The mausoleum offers her,
Madame decides that, to pursue Monsieur,
Starvation is her best expedient:
    Portal direct, through which to quit
This mortal coil and be well rid of it.
    One day… Then two… And she had fed
On nought but her "alas"es and "ah me"s:
Long song of woe; duly dispirited,
    Cursing the gods, fate's vagaries,
And all of life's most grave inequities.

    Now, hard by where Monsieur lay dead,
A second corpse hung swinging in the breeze:
    A proper blackguard, and for whom
Only the gibbet—no fine marble tomb—
Would stand to mark his infamous demise;
Left thus, so other thieves might cast their eyes
    Thereon, and be thereby deterred.

C'étoit trop de severité:
Mais la publique utilité
Défendoit que l'on fist au Garde aucune grace.
Pendant la nuit il vid aux fentes du tombeau
Briller quelque clarté, spectacle assez nouveau.
Curieux, il y court, entend de loin la Dame
Remplissant l'air de ses clameurs.
Il entre, est étonné, demande à cette femme
Pourquoi ces cris, pourquoi ces pleurs,
Pourquoi cette triste musique,
Pourquoi cette maison noire et mélancolique?
Occupée à ses pleurs, à peine elle entendit
Toutes ces demandes frivoles.
Le mort pour elle y répondit:
Cet objet sans autres paroles
Disoit assez par quel malheur
La Dame s'enterroit ainsi toute vivante.
Nous avons fait serment, ajoûta la Suivante,
De nous laisser mourir de faim et de douleur.
Encor que le Soldat fût mauvais Orateur,
Il leur fit concevoir ce que c'est que la vie.
La Dame cette fois eut de l'attention;
Et déja l'autre passion
Se trouvoit un peu ralentie:
Le tems avoit agi. Si la foi du serment,
Poursuivit le Soldat, vous défend l'aliment,
Voïez-moi manger seulement,
Vous n'en mourrez pas moins. Un tel temperament
Ne déplut pas aux deux femelles.
Conclusion, qu'il obtint d'elles
Une permission d'apporter son soupé:
Ce qu'il fit. Et l'Esclave eut le cœur fort tenté
De renoncer dés-lors à la cruelle envie
De tenir au mort compagnie.
Madame, ce dit-elle, un penser m'est venu:
Qu'importe à vôtre Epoux que vous cessiez de vivre?
Croïez-vous que lui-même il fût homme à vous suivre
Si par vôtre trépas vous l'aviez prevenu?
Non, Madame, il voudroit achever sa carriere.
La nôtre sera longue encor, si nous voulons.
Se faut-il, à vingt ans, enfermer dans la biere?
Nous aurons tout loisir d'habiter ces maisons,

A soldier, placed to guard this gallows-bird,
Well paid therefor, did so with anxious care.
    For if, through his neglect—mayhap
    The merest nod or briefest nap—
    Brigands or friends or kin should dare
Come snatch the corpse, then must it be replaced
    By him himself, and that posthaste!
(Punishment most severe, but one that would
Presumably best serve the common good.)
And so it happens that, indeed, that night
    Said guard espies a beam of light
Slivering through the gloom. Great his surprise
As to the tomb he hies him; stops; hears cries
    Rending the air… Inside he goes:
    Astonished at the sight, he eyes
The grieving widow there, bawling her woes.
    Many his wherefores and his whys:
Why such? Why so?… But so distraught is she
    That she ignores his queries, lets
    The corpse, in mute soliloquy,
Account for her vociferous regrets
And her decision thus to be entombed.
Her slave adds more: "Madame and I are doomed
To starve with grief. For so we swore." Whereat
    The guard, distressed at their condition,
Discourses—though no gilt-tongued rhetorician—
    On life (its meaning, and all that).
The wife gives ear, more willing by the minute;
Hears what he has to say, takes pleasure in it;
Begins to lose her firm resolve… Says he:
    "Starve if you must. I'll not entreat you.
    But if you sit and watch me eat, you
    Need die no less, I guarantee.
Pray let me fetch my supper." They agree;
And off he goes, returning with his food.
    As thus he supped and chomped and chewed,
The slave began to harbor much misgiving
    About the cruel vicissitude
Of thus departing from amongst the living
To join Monsieur in death. "Madame," she said,
"The thought occurs to me that, were you dead
And were your husband yet alive, then surely

On ne meurt que trop tôt: qui nous presse? attendons.
Quant à moy je voudrois ne mourir que ridée.
Voulez-vous emporter vos appas chez les morts?
Que vous servira-t-il d'en être regardée?
   Tantôt en voïant les tresors
Dont le Ciel prit plaisir d'orner vôtre visage,
   Je disois: Helas! c'est dommage!
Nous mêmes nous allons enterrer tout cela.
A ce discours flateur la Dame s'éveilla.
Le Dieu qui fait aimer prit son temps; il tira
Deux traits de son carquois: de l'un il entama
Le Soldat jusqu'au vif; l'autre effleura la Dame.
Jeune et belle, elle avoit sous ses pleurs de l'éclat!
   Et des gens de goût délicat
Auroient bien pû l'aimer, et même êtant leur femme.
Le Garde en fut épris; les pleurs et la pitié,
   Sorte d'amours aïant ses charmes,
Tout y fit: une belle, alors qu'elle est en larmes
   En est plus belle de moitié.
Voilà donc nôtre Veuve écoutant la loüange,
Poison qui de l'amour est le premier degré;
   La voilà qui trouve à son gré
Celui qui le lui donne; il fait tant qu'elle mange;
Il fait tant que de plaire, et se rend en effet
Plus digne d'être aimé que le mort le mieux fait.
   Il fait tant enfin qu'elle change;
Et toûjours par degrez, comme l'on peut penser,
De l'un à l'autre il fait cette femme passer:
   Je ne le trouve pas etrange.
Elle écoute un Amant, elle en fait un Mari,
Le tout au nez du mort qu'elle avoit tant cheri.
Pendant cet hymenée, un voleur se hazarde
D'enlever le dépôt commis aux soins du Garde:
Il en entend le bruit, il y court à grands pas;
   Mais en vain, la chose étoit faite.
Il revient au tombeau conter son embarras,
   Ne sçachant où trouver retraite.
L'Esclave alors lui dit, le voïant éperdu:
   L'on vous a pris vôtre pendu?
Les Loix ne vous feront, dites-vous, nulle grace?
Si Madame y consent, j'y remedîrai bien.
   Mettons nôtre mort en la place.

There's little question, *entre nous,*
But that he'd not be quick to follow you.
Life is so short: why leave it prematurely?
At twenty years the grave can wait, no worry!
Long will it be our host: so why the hurry?
Me? Let me live till wrinkles fill my face!
What? Would you waste your beauty and your grace
Upon the dead? What pleasures can they give them,
 Imprisoned in their chill embrace?
 Better to let yourself outlive them—
These charms divine of yours—and not allow
The jealous bier too soon to claim them." Now,
The compliments, of course, have their effect:
Madame is quickened, as you might expect,
To thoughts of beauty and, perforce, of love.
 At length, the impish god thereof
Looses an arrow from his quiver at her,
 And at the guard as well. The latter,
Pierced to the heart, is smitten utterly—
 More deeply than, at first, is she.
The more she sobs, the more those teardrops flatter
The winsome face behind the weeping mask.
(Beauty that even many a husband would
 Find worth the yoke of husbandhood!)
And so the soldier, warming to the task,
 Proceeds to woo the widow, doing
 Everything wooers do a-wooing,
Much to the pleasure of Madame the wooed.
He does so well that, soon, she tastes his food;
So well, that he seems fitter, far, to have her
Than even the most fair and fit cadaver;
So well, that there, before her dear deceased,
Widow turns wife—or so to speak, at least.
But as they lie thus consummating, lo!
A brigand steals that other corpse—the one
Our groom forgets to guard... He'll run... But no,
 Too late, alack! The deed is done...
Back to the tomb, in panic, will he flee
To tell Madame the fell catastrophe.
How can he save his skin? Aye, that's the question!
For which the slave girl, full of sympathy,
 Offers him an untoward suggestion:

Les passans n'y connoîtront rien.
La Dame y consentit. O volages femelles!
La femme est toûjours femme; il en est qui sont belles;
        Il en est qui ne le sont pas.
        S'il en étoit d'assez fideles,
        Elles auroient assez d'apas.

Prudes, vous vous devez défier de vos forces.
Ne vous vantez de rien. Si vôtre intention
        Est de resister aux amorces,
La nôtre est bonne aussi: mais l'execution
Nous trompe également; témoin cette Matrone.
        Et n'en déplaise au bon Petrone,
Ce n'étoit pas un fait tellement merveilleux,
Qu'il en dût proposer l'exemple à nos neveux.
Cette Veuve n'eut tort qu'au bruit qu'on lui vid faire,
Qu'au dessein de mourir mal conçû, mal formé:
        Car de mettre au patibulaire
        Le corps d'un mari tant aimé,
Ce n'étoit pas peut-être une si grande affaire;
Cela lui sauvoit l'autre: et tout consideré,
Mieux vaut Goujat debout qu'Empereur enterré.

"By Madame's leave, no one will know if we
Hang up our corpse to take your corpse's place."
Madame agrees… O woman! Fickle race!
    Some fair; some plain of face and feature;
But faithful? Ah, would there were such a creature!

Prudes, be advised: vaunt not your strength of will
Though your intent be to resist temptation.
    For, fare we well or fare we ill,
    Strong, too, is man's determination.
    Witness our famous Matron, who—
Meaning the good Petronius no offense—
Did, I must say, what many a wife would do
Under the circumstances; and who, hence,
    Deserves no exemplary mention.
Her folly? Vowing in her innocence,
    To die entombed: absurd intention!
    Nor need she have too long repented
Hanging her dear-departed late-lamented
To save her swain. For, as she would discover,
    Better to have a living lover—
Even a varlet, poor and lowly bred—
Than all your kings and emperors, rich but dead.

(XII, 26)

NOTES

The Lion and the Rat and The Dove and the Ant

1. Generations of critics have noted that this concluding line seems curiously out of place, introducing a second moral apparently unrelated to the one announced in the opening quatrain and illustrated by both fables. Henri Regnier, in his exhaustively annotated edition, explains it away as merely a typical passing reflection, unconnected to what precedes or follows. (See his *Œuvres de J. de la Fontaine,* rev. ed. [Paris: Hachette, 1883–92], 11, 163.) But La Fontaine does seem to be suggesting, albeit vaguely, that the virtues of patience and hard work are, after all, ones that the small and weak are, by their very nature, obliged to display. Without presuming to second-guess him—or to contradict the learned Regnier—I offer a translation that, with a minor liberty, assumes that to have been La Fontaine's intent.

2. Antiquity's association of the dove with Venus is recorded in a number of works, among them Ovid's *Metamorphoses* (xv, 386), where "Cytherea's dove" figures in a brief listing of those birds especially dear to certain gods.

The Crow Who Wanted to Imitate the Eagle

1. Polyphemus the Cyclops, villain of Book ix of *The Odyssey* and later works of Homeric inspiration—and, perhaps not coincidentally, himself a shepherd—is, in his many graphic representations, always heavily bearded, a characteristic consistent with his persona in Euripides' satyr play *Cyclops*.

The Wolf Turned Shepherd

1. Guillot, the name La Fontaine chooses—here and in many other fables—for his hero (and antihero), is one of the many typically bucolic and pastoral names common since the Middle Ages. This one is especially appropriate, given the fictitious, allusive existence, in the sixteenth century, of one "Guillot le menteur" ("Guillot the liar"). (See Edmond Huguet, *Dictionnaire de la langue française du seizième siècle,* iv, 411.) Interesting too is the fact that La Fontaine considers the word he uses to characterize his sham Guillot—*sycophante*—uncommon enough to require a footnote, defining it as *trompeur* ("deceiver"). The word is, in fact, attested at least as early as the preceding century.

The Fox and the Goat

1. The punctuational imprecision of the original makes it unclear whether this last line is spoken by the wolf or, characteristically, by the moralizing La Fontaine. Both possibilities make equally good sense. I have opted for the latter since it gives me the excuse to give two proverbs for the price of one.

The Miser Who Lost His Treasure

1. The allusion is, of course, to the Cynic philosopher Diogenes (ca. 412–323 B.C.), celebrated for his quest for "the honest man," whose contempt for his age led him to divest himself of all the comforts of life and live in a tub.

2. The fable referred to figures as number 225 of the "Fabulæ Græcæ" in Ben Edwin Perry, *Æsopica* (Urbana: University of Illinois Press, 1952; rpt., New York: Arno Press, 1980), p. 409.

The Snake and the File

1. Curiously, La Fontaine's classical and medieval predecessors had made the snake's neighbor a locksmith. (See, *inter alia,* my *Fables from Old French: Æsop's Beasts and Bumpkins* [Middletown, Conn.: Wesleyan University Press, 1982], pp. 112–13.) Perhaps he made the change from *serrurier* to *horloger* to permit his biting allusion to "the teeth of Time" (below). Or perhaps the allusion grew out of the change. At any rate, for those more accustomed to the sound of "locksmith," "clocksmith" at least provides a serendipitous echo.

The Lion Going Off to War

1. Readers given to zoological precision will, I hope, excuse my liberty here in transforming the hare into a rabbit—all the more appropriate in the context, I think, since the latter is even less ferocious than the former. Besides, La Fontaine too, on occasion, sacrifices on the altar of easy rhyme.

The Bear and the Two Companions

1. The reference is to Rabelais's celebrated sheep-merchant, in *Pantagruel* (IV, ch. 8), likewise done in, though in a different manner.

2. Though it no doubt owes its popularity to La Fontaine, like many others, the proverb "Il ne faut pas vendre la peau de l'ours avant de l'avoir tué" ("You mustn't sell the bear's skin before you kill him"), equivalent to "Don't count your chickens before they're hatched," dates from at least as far back as the fifteenth century. (See Adrien Jean Victor Le Roux de Lincy, *Le Livre des proverbes français,* 2 vols. [Paris: Delahay, 1859], II, 191.)

The Ass Dressed in the Lion's Skin

1. La Fontaine's irony here is obvious. He gives his peasant miller a name—Martin—traditionally applied in French to the ass, as, for example, in the proverb "Il y a (à la foire) plus d'un âne qui s'appelle Martin," usually translated as the less-than-common "There are more Jacks than one at the fair." His irony is not original, however. It should be remembered that the same name is given to the peasant in the proverb "Faute d'un point Martin perdit son âne" ("For want of a nail the shoe was lost").

2. Readers familiar with the more common antique meaning of the noun *équipage* ("horse and carriage") may take issue with my translation here. In La Fontaine's lexicon, however, and that of many of his contemporaries, it is frequently used to mean "attire," as the present context suggests.

The Mule Who Boasted of His Family Tree

ILLUSTRATION: The image is an homage to an etching by Francisco Goya from his collection *Los Caprichos* [Madrid, 1799], which bears the caption "Asta su Abuelo" ("Back to His Grandfather"). The image seemed such a perfect summation of the title of this fable, that I made a drawing after the etching on the left and one of Goya proofing that plate on the right. Making images "after" paintings is part of the history of printmaking; it seemed only appropriate for one printmaker to pay respect to another. (D.S.)

The Old Man and the Ass

1. La Fontaine's last phrase ("... *en bon François*") may confuse those readers unfamiliar with seventeenth-century orthography and sometimes capricious capitalization. Suffice it to say that *François,* here, is not the modern proper name but merely his period's spelling of the adjective *français,* applied in this phrase to the language.

The Ass and His Masters

1. Purists may well prefer "currier" to "tanner," the two not being synonyms and the former being a more exact translation of the French *corroyeur*. I prefer "tanner," with no detriment to the meaning, since, when read aloud, in many English dialects, the somewhat archaic "currier" might not only not be understood but might be misconstrued as "courier."

2. As for any equally punctilious readers who may object to my rhyming liberty here ("indict 'em / *ad infinitum*"), I urge them—invite 'em—to recall Jonathan Swift's celebrated lines from *On Poetry* (1733):

So Nat'ralists observe, a Flea
Hath smaller fleas that on him prey;
And these have smaller fleas to bite 'em,
And so proceed, *ad infinitum*.

The Peasant and the Snake

1. I choose to avoid the obvious problem of how to translate La Fontaine's designation of the snake here as an *insecte,* a literal rendition of which would sound curious in English. The poet was neither zoologically naïve nor misinformed. He was, on the contrary, respecting the etymology of the word (from the Latin, *insectum,* "cut into sections"), commonly applied in the seventeenth century, according to *Le Grand Robert,* to animals like worms, snakes, *et al.,* that, according to popular belief, continued to live for a time after being cut in two.

The Sick Lion and the Fox

ILLUSTRATION: The subject of the sick and aging lion is a common one, recurring in this collection three times. This fable and "The Lion, the Wolf, and the Fox" both recall the woodcut illustrations of the fifteenth-century German block book *Der Kranke Lewe (The Sick Lion),* probably printed in Basel in 1458. I have here tried to echo this style in homage to this incunabulum of printed book illustration. (D.S.)

The Animals Ill with the Plague

1. The Acheron, it will be remembered, was, like the Styx, one of the five rivers of Hades. From the Greek for "river of sorrows," it is mentioned by Milton in *Paradise Lost:* "Sad Acheron of sorrow, black and deep" (II, 578).

The Vultures and the Pigeons

1. The reference, as in "The Dove and the Ant," is to the dove (see p. 155, note 2), not only the sacred bird of Venus, according to Ovid, but also, as he tells us in the *Metamorphoses* (XIV, 597)—though without specifying the intermediary of a chariot—a means of her divine locomotion.

2. The allusion to Prometheus's optimism, in the face of his persistent liver-plucking enemy's seeming imminent demise, is too obvious to require explanation. Readers who do not understand it will find it amply elucidated in Æschylus's *Prometheus Bound.*

3. This fable is designated as number 8 of Book VII in those collections where a pair of preceding fables, "Le Héron" and "La Fille" (not translated here), are presented each with a separate number rather than in tandem. (The disparity is, of course, continued throughout the succeeding fables of the same book.)

The Coach and the Fly

1. Obviously, I take the liberty of offering here an interpretation of La Fontaine's line that not everyone will agree with. It was the late Professor Ted Morris who, years ago, first suggested to me (and other then students) that, flies being flies and horses being horses, the only appropriate payment for the hero(ine) of this fable would, indeed, be the latters' droppings. I've always thought he was right.

2. See p. 160, note 3.

The Two Cocks

ILLUSTRATION: Here I turn to the Japanese master woodblock artist Hokusai (1760–1849) for a model. Paired and (usually) fighting cocks appear many times in his *Manga* (sketch books or pattern books used as models by many other artists). One of the most famous images from the *Manga* turns the cocks into demons who share certain features of humans and crows but who fight like roosters. I also looked at the double-panel print by Utamaro of himself painting a cock in a mural in the *Annals of the Green Houses* (1804). (D.S.)

1. The Trojan river, the Xanthos, also known as the Scamander, would figure in one of La Fontaine's more cynical tales, "Le Fleuve Scamandre," in his *Contes et nouvelles en vers*. (See my *La Fontaine's Bawdy: Of Libertines, Louts, and Lechers* [Princeton: Princeton University Press, 1992], pp. 252–59.) It was dubbed the Xanthos ("golden red") by Homer, for reasons variously hypothesized by Pliny and others. As we are told in *The Iliad,* the gods referred to by La Fontaine were Venus and Mars, wounded by Diomedes (V, 330ff., 855ff.), and Mars, later struck down by Minerva (XXI, 385ff.).

2. See p. 160, note 3.

The Lion, the Wolf, and the Fox

1. The reference is clearly to the ceremonial nightly retirings of Louis XIV (*les couchers du roi*), which, like his daily arisings (*les levers*), were typically pompous events attended by the most important members of the royal household, intimates, and favored dignitaries. Readers wishing details of these complexly orchestrated examples of the Sun King's self-infatuation may consult many sources; among them the mammoth *La Grande Encyclopédie*, 31 vols. (Paris: La Société Anonyme de la Grande Encylopédie, *et al.*, 1886–1902), XIII, 29–30; XXII, 135.

The Lioness's Funeral

1. La Fontaine's versification here is rather curious in that, in the lines immediately preceding (11 through 20 of the original), he resorts three

times to a series of three successive uses of the same rhyme (*trouva / aban-donna / résonna; Courtisans / gens / indifferens; estre / parêtre / maître*). This three-rhyme phenomenon, which doesn't appear to serve any particular artistic purpose, is occasionally met with in his work, but never, to my knowledge, in such a concentrated dose. Considering it something of an inexplicable aberration, I have seen no reason to duplicate it.

2. La Fontaine combines two references from *Proverbs*: XVI, 14 and XX, 2.

The Ape and the Leopard

1. La Fontaine uses the names Gille and Bertrand several times for his various monkeys. The former, possibly akin to the Old French *gilain* ("trickster"), personifying fraud and deceit as early as the medieval *Roman de Renart,* later would come to suggest simplicity, no doubt from the name of the popular seventeenth-century clown Gilles le Niais. The latter has no specific connotations that I know of, though La Fontaine himself uses it elsewhere with the ecclesiastical title *Dom* ("Du Thésauriseur et du Singe" [XII, 3]). That being the case, and following the context here, I have taken the minor liberty of doing likewise.

The Treasure and the Two Men

1. There is some disagreement regarding the origin of the proverbial expression "loger le diable dans sa bourse" to indicate utter poverty. The tireless lexicographer Littré accepted its attribution to the Renaissance poet Mellin de Saint-Gelais, though casting some doubt by citing an Italian equivalent. (See his four-volume *Dictionnaire de la langue française* [Paris: Hachette, 1881–82], under *diable,* II, 1146.) Another explanation suggests an origin based on the fact that early coins were struck with an image of the cross, obviously antithetical to the devil. (See P. M. Quitard, *Dictionnaire étymologique, historique et anecdotique des proverbes et des locutions proverbiales de la langue française* [Paris: P. Bertrand, 1842], pp. 309–10.) One way or the other, it is clear that, unlike several of the proverbs in La Fontaine's *Fables*, this one considerably antedates his use.

2. After much translatory soul-searching I decided on the present lines rather than my first choice, to wit:

> and found
> The treasure, object of his concupiscing,
> Missing.

Although the verb "to concupisce" seems never to have been documented (at least according to the OED), the adjective "concupiscible" would, I think, have justified its use. That solution, however, struck me, for all its virtues, as something of an overtranslation in light of La Fontaine's extreme simplicity, and I abandoned it, albeit reluctantly.

The Man and the Snake

1. La Fontaine's somewhat convoluted musing—attributable to the ox's style, as ponderous as his person—seems to suggest that here, as in "Le Coche et la Mouche" (see p. 161, note 1), we are dealing with a quadruped's only concrete form of remuneration—in a "manure" of speaking, that is.

The Money-Burier and His Friend

1. The French *enfouisseur* ("burier") is, to say the least, an uncommon noun and was equally so in La Fontaine's time. Dictionaries that include it at all usually cite the present fable to authenticate it. That being the case, I have taken a minor liberty with my English version of the title, since the simple "The Burier and His Friend" would hardly denote what the poet intended.

2. This passage, with its indisputable but self-evident digression, is not one of the many studied in a curious little volume of economics-related passages culled from the *Fables*. But the many that are discussed show to what extent La Fontaine was, at least superficially, concerned with monetary matters. (See Gustave Boissonade, *La Fontaine économiste* [Paris: Guillaumin, 1872].) For a more telling example, see "The Value of Knowledge," my translation of "L'Avantage de la science," in *Fifty Fables of La Fontaine* (Urbana: University of Illinois Press, 1988), p. 91 and pp. 117–18, note 1.

The Old Man and the Three Young Men

1. This curiously self-referential conclusion was much admired by the eighteenth-century moralist Chamfort, who saw it as a rare example of the aging La Fontaine's artistic self-effacement before impending death. La Fontaine, more concerned with the message than with the medium, passes himself off not as the author of the tale but merely the transcriber of the old man's memorial inscription. (See Regnier's edition, XII, 159-60.) Regarding that inscription, we must be willing to suspend disbelief: given the length of the story, the cenotaph on which it was supposedly engraved would have to be rather large. To be sure, La Fontaine's source (Abstemius, 167: "De viro decrepito arbores inserente") is somewhat shorter, thanks both to the pithy terseness of Latin and to the fact that, in that version, there is only one man instead of three.

The Fox, the Flies, and the Hedgehog

1. This appearance of the hedgehog in La Fontaine's *dramatis animalia*, as he confides in a typically personal aside, was indeed the first of his corpus. Unless, that is, one considers a prior version of the present fable, unpublished during his lifetime, cited by various scholars,

Regnier among them (see his *Œuvres de J. de la Fontaine*, rev. ed. [Paris: Hachette, 1883-92], III, 266-67). Though he obviously didn't know it at the time, it would also be the only one.

2. La Fontaine was not, by any means, the first to adapt this political apologue from Aristotle's *Rhetoric* (II, 20), one with a particularly rich history. It would show up, for example, several centuries after Aristotle, in Flavius Josephus, *Antiquities of the Jews* (XVIII, VI, 5) and eventually in a variety of Spanish exemplary tales based on the *Gesta Romanorum*. For the work of one of La Fontaine's more important French predecessors, the sixteenth-century fabulist Philibert Guide (a.k.a. Philibert Hégémon), as well as other incarnations before and after, see my collection *The Fabulists French: Verse Fables of Nine Centuries* (Urbana: University of Illinois Press, 1992), pp. 28-29.

The Forest and the Woodsman

1. One should not exaggerate La Fontaine's seemingly proto-environmentalist defense of nature, evident here, as in many of his more "philosophical" fables. Much has been written on it; but, although it is more probably something of a pastoral literary conceit more common among his immediate predecessors—Racan, Théophile de Viau, Tristan L'Hermite, *et al.*—than among his citified contemporaries, it is at least based on personal experience. Recall that, as a child, La Fontaine delighted in accompanying his father on his woodland rounds about his native Château-Thierry as Maître des Eaux et Forêts ("Master of the Waters and Forests")—roughly the equivalent of a forest warden cum conservationist—and that La Fontaine himself inherited that position as a young adult. (See, *inter alia*, Philip Wadsworth, *Young La Fontaine* [Evanston, Ill.: Northwestern University Press, 1952], pp. 16-21.)

The Fox, the Wolf, and the Horse

1. La Fontaine's concluding line, meaning literally "The wise man distrusts every stranger," certainly smacks of a proverb and may well have preexisted his use of it here, though I find no evidence of it in this form. In fact, sources usually cite this line as its origin; and it surely wouldn't be the only one of his to pass into proverbial usage. Perhaps La Fontaine was expressing, in different dress, the then common proverb "Défiance est mère de sûreté" ("Distrust is mother of security"); one whose cynical message was criticized by his contemporary, the churchman-littérateur Bossuet, who said of it: "J'aime beaucoup mieux être trompé que de vivre éternellement dans la défiance" ("I should rather be deceived than to live eternally in distrust"). (See P. M. Quitard, *Dictionnaire étymologique, historique et anecdotique des proverbes et des locutions proverbiales de la langue française* [Paris: P. Bertrand, 1842], p. 291.)

The Fox and the Young Turkey Cocks

1. The turkey had been introduced into Europe from North America as early as the sixteenth century. In France, in La Fontaine's time, one distinguished between the full-grown *dindon* ("turkey cock," the male of the *dinde*) and the young *poulet d'Inde,* which today would more usually be termed the *dindonneau.* All the words carry (and carried) with them the connotation of stupidity, for which the turkey is, perhaps unjustly, famous.

2. My phrase "fowl cohort," echoing one above, is not a misprint. The pun, not in the original, is my attempt to suggest something of the La Fontaine playfulness inherent in his typical coinage *la dindonnière gent,* roughly translatable as "turkeydom."

3. One tends to think of the pseudoscientific work of the eighteenth-century physician Franz Mesmer—he of "animal magnetism" fame—as the beginnings of modern concern with hypnotism and such, though the ancients (and even the primitives) were well aware of the phenomenon of "fascination," of which the fox's ploy is a rudimentary example. It may have been suggested to La Fontaine by chapter VI ("De scientia brutorum") of Thomas Willis's treatise *De Anima brutorum quæ Hominis vitalis ac sensitiva est exercitationes duæ* (London, 1672), a lengthy passage of which is found in Henri Regnier's *Œuvres de J. de la Fontaine,* rev. ed. [Paris: Hachette, 1883–92], III, 405–6.

4. The reference is, of course, to Harlequin (or Arlequin), the French descendant of the Italian Arlecchino, one of the stock characters of the *commedia dell'arte,* known for his improvisational talents, most often used to extricate his masters from a variety of entanglements, and usually not without a goodly dose of self-interest. Of his many incarnations in the French theater—under the same or other names—the most famous and well developed is Beaumarchais's celebrated Figaro.

The Scythian Philosopher

ILLUSTRATION: The curious and very particular costume of the Scythian is based on a drawing from an Attic red-figure cup painting from the Museo Nazionale, Naples, reproduced in Wm. Blake Tyrrell, *Amazons* (Baltimore: Johns Hopkins University Press, 1984), title page; and more directly from a golden comb and golden bottle pictured in *From the Lands of the Scythians: Ancient Treasures from the Museums of the U.S.S.R.* (New York: Metropolitan Museum of Art, 1975) plate 13 and plates 17, 18. (D.S.)

1. The reference is to the old man from Corycia, in the *Georgics* (IV, 127–33), who, "spacing herbs among his thickets, / And setting out white lilies, slender poppies, / And vervain, felt sure that his riches

matched / The wealth of kings . . ." (See *Virgil's "Georgics,"* trans. Smith Palmer Bovie [Chicago: University of Chicago Press, 1956], p. 90.)

The Elephant and Jupiter's Ape

1. See p. 162, note 1.

2. It is tempting to see here a wry suggestion on La Fontaine's part—coming full circle at the end of his collection and, indeed, his life—that even the ant, arrogantly provident as he depicts her in his earliest fable, "La Cigale et la Fourmi" (I, 1), can run afoul of circumstances and need Jupiter's help.

3. As for the final couplet—a somewhat feeble ending to an otherwise powerful fable—I have chosen to interpret it with a rather more ironic twist than La Fontaine perhaps intended: the elephant's size will not deter divine concern even if it does not guarantee it either.

The Matron of Ephesus

1. This work—obviously, by its length and *dramatis personæ*, much more a tale than a fable, properly speaking—figures, in fact, in most editions of La Fontaine's *Contes et nouvelles en vers*. It was originally published in 1682 and dates from at least a year earlier. Its inclusion in Book XII of the *Fables*, published in 1693 (along with "Belphégor," also a *conte*), is incongruous, to say the least. Be that as it may, the story, taken from Petronius's *Satyricon* (CXI–CXII), was a favorite of many authors, both pre- and post-La Fontaine. (The poet himself would seem to have been inspired by it years before, at least obliquely, in "La Jeune Veuve" [VI, 21], itself also more a *conte* than a fable.) The present translation appears also in my collection *La Fontaine's Bawdy: Of Libertines, Louts, and Lechers* (Princeton: Princeton University Press, 1992). The tale is not included in the Regnier edition of the *Fables*.

2. La Fontaine's reference, mildly deformed in my version, is to the family from which the pretentious Madame de Sotenville proudly claims descent in Molière's comedy *Georges Dandin*.

3. My seemingly unorthodox use of a single rhyme over three consecutive lines is justified by several instances of the same curious phenomenon in La Fontaine himself, among them his own example here, a dozen lines below (*lieux / mieux / yeux*).

A Note on the Translator

NORMAN R. SHAPIRO, recognized as one of the leading translators of French verse, prose, and theater, holds the B.A., M.A., and Ph.D. from Harvard University and, as Fulbright Scholar, the Diplôme de Langue et Lettres Françaises from the Université d'Aix-Marseille. He is Professor of Romance Languages and Literatures at Wesleyan University, where he teaches a variety of courses in French theater, poety, and Black Francophone literature, as well as American Sign Language. Among his published works are *Four Farces by Georges Feydeau,* a National Book Award nominee in translation; *Négritude: Black Poetry from Africa and the Caribbean; The Comedy of Eros: Medieval French Guides to the Art of Love,* prepared with a Ford Foundation Grant from the National Translation Center, University of Texas, and recipient of several awards; *Kamouraska,* by Quebec novelist Anne Hébert; Jean Raspail's controversial novel *The Camp of the Saints; Fables from Old French: Æsop's Beasts and Bumpkins,* selected by *Choice* as an Academic Book of the Year; *Fifty Fables of La Fontaine; The Fabulists French: Verse Fables of Nine Centuries,* recognized by the American Literary Translators Association as an Outstanding Book of the Year; and *La Fontaine's Bawdy: Of Libertines, Louts, and Lechers,* a PEN–Book-of-the-Month-Club Award nominee. He is currently at work on a collection of verse translations from Baudelaire's *Les Fleurs du mal.* His adaptations of Georges Feydeau and other French comic dramatists are published in several volumes, among them *A Flea in Her Rear, or Ants in Her Pants, and Other Vintage French Farces,* and are frequently performed in this country, Canada, and abroad.

A Note on the Illustrator

DAVID SCHORR is a printmaker, painter, and sometime book designer. He shows regularly at the Mary Ryan Gallery in New York City, where he maintains a studio. His B.A. is from Brown and his B.F.A. and M.F.A. are from Yale. He is Professor of Art at Wesleyan University, where he teaches printmaking, typography, and drawing. Books he has illustrated include *Parallel Lives,* by Phyllis Rose; *No Witnesses,* by Paul Monette; as well as two others with Norman Shapiro: *The Fabulists French* and *La Fontaine's Bawdy.* He is currently making eighteen engravings for Norman Shapiro's new translation of selections from *Les Fleurs du mal.* His portraits of writers, artists, and musicians have graced the literary section of *The New Republic* for many years. His work can be found in numerous public and private collections, including the Boston Museum of Fine Arts, the New York Public Library, the National Gallery of Art, the Fogg Museum, the Israel Museum in Jerusalem, and the Cleveland Museum of Art. A fellow at the Calcografia Nazionale in Rome for some years, he likes to work in far-flung places, having made many prints at Tamarind Institute in New Mexico, at Penland in the mountains of North Carolina, and most recently serving as a visiting professor at the National Institute of Design in Ahmedabad, India.